Set down your selfie stick and pick up this book instead! *#Struggles* is a must-read for anyone who feels enslaved to technology—and let's face it, don't we all? Craig Groeschel's masterful blend of storytelling, humor, and biblical truth make this his most compelling and thought-provoking book to date. I can't think of a more relevant message for my generation as we navigate life and love in today's digital world.

—Austin, age 25

In a world where we're often drowning in demands and constantly connected to social media, Craig offers a refreshing relief from the madness. You will finish his new book, *#Struggles*, feeling encouraged by tools you can use every day to embrace life instead of being consumed by it. This book is a gift to our generation!

—Michelle, age 29

Having phones, tablets, and computers at our fingertips can be amazing, but it also causes plenty of #struggles in our lives. In his new book, Craig gives us some practical suggestions to help us in the advanced, technological society in which we live. You won't hear him tell us to discard the techie toys we've grown to love, but we will be challenged to put our devices in their rightful place. Pick up this book now and #endthestruggle!

—Cindy, age 45

I may not be in the digital generation, but the #struggle is real for me too! Craig's important book *#Struggles* inspired me to take a long break from social media. I deleted the apps from my phone for a few months to reset my behaviors. If you need a reset, you will definitely want to pick up *#Struggles*.

—Kendra, age 42

There's not a person alive who doesn't need to push the reset button in life from time to time. Craig's amazing book gets straight to the heart of the #struggles we all face using humor and practical suggestions to get us on track and stay on track.

—Dana, age 36

We can all agree that technology and social media can be used in powerful ways to accomplish amazing things. We also recognize that the #struggles Craig Groeschel outlines in his latest book can be equally destructive. Never fear! Craig shares with us how to use technology and social media in a positive way while maintaining authenticity and engaging in real-life relationships and opportunities to make a difference. Whether you are sixteen or sixty, Craig's humor and transparency will inspire you to apply some of the practical tips he suggests for striking a balance in our use of social media.

—Allyson, age 47

Craig Groeschel's book *#Struggles* is easily the best book written about being a follower of Christ on social media. If you've ever felt like everyone except you has it all together, put your smartphone on silent and start reading *#Struggles*.

—Jordan, age 20

Pastor Craig has a finger on my generation's pulse: many of us live vicariously through laptop screens instead of living victoriously through Christ. This book touches a nerve that didn't even exist a decade ago. If you're on social media, put down the phone and start reading *#Struggles*.

—Chuck, age 26

I stare at my screen and I feel less. Less than I am, less than I want to be, and less than I was created to be. Is the technology to blame? No. Do I need help balancing the power it holds for me and others? Absolutely. Enter *#Struggles*, a much-needed book for anyone who spends time online.

—Lori, age 45

I'll never forget when my university got Facebook years ago. It's been part of my life ever since. Reading Groeschel's book *#Struggles* will help you understand the place social media should have in your life. This book is definitely a must-read for Millennials.

—Jess, age 31

With the advancement of social media, it's become easier than ever to connect with people around the world. If we're not careful, these online interactions can become more of a priority than the people right around us. In *#Struggles*, Craig Groeschel shares great principles that helped me look beyond the gadget in my hand to fully engage with the people in my life in a way that honors both God and them. Everyone who has a smart device needs to read this book!

—Amanda, age 44

No matter your age or stage of life, you can't deny that social media is changing the world we live in, and Pastor Craig makes the connection for how it's changing each of us. Our #struggles are real, and this book gives this generation timely advice on how to keep our eyes fixed on Christ instead of being trapped by a screen.

—Lucinda, age 30

It seems like my whole world is wrapped up in what my friends are doing online. I've always felt empty but didn't know why. Craig's new book, *#Struggles*, woke me up to admit that I really am addicted to social media and worry way too much about what other people think. Because of this book, I'm going to get closer to Jesus, and I believe it will help you too.

—McKae, age 14

#struggles

Share your thoughts about this book on social media using the hashtag #strugglesbook.

OTHER BOOKS BY CRAIG GROESCHEL

Altar Ego: Becoming Who God Says You Are

Chazown: Define Your Vision, Pursue Your Passion, Live Your Life on Purpose

The Christian Atheist: Believing in God but Living as If He Doesn't Exist

Dare to Drop the Pose (previously titled *Confessions of a Pastor*)

Fight: Winning the Battles That Matter Most

From This Day Forward: Five Commitments to Fail-Proof Your Marriage (with Amy Groeschel)

It: How Churches and Leaders Can Get It and Keep It

Love, Sex, and Happily Ever After (previously titled *Going All the Way*)

Soul Detox: Clean Living in a Contaminated World

Weird: Because Normal Isn't Working

What Is God Really Like? (general editor)

#struggles

Following Jesus in a Selfie-Centered World

Craig Groeschel ✔

ZONDERVAN

#Struggles

Copyright © 2015 by Craig Groeschel

Requests for information should be addressed to:
Zondervan, 3900 *Sparks Dr. SE, Grand Rapids, Michigan 49546*

ISBN 978-0-310-34886-3 (hardcover)

ISBN 978-0-310-34309-7 (international trade paper edition)

ISBN 978-0-310-34573-2 (audio)

ISBN 978-0-310-34293-9 (ebook)

Craig Groeschel is represented by Thomas J. Winters of Winters & King, Inc., Tulsa, Oklahoma.

Cover design: *Dual Identity*
Cover photography: © svetikd / iStockphoto®
Interior design: *Kait Lamphere*

First printing August 2015 / Printed in the United States of America

This book is for everyone who refuses to worship something that never satisfies. May you experience more of him.

He must become greater; I must become less (John 3:30).

CONTENTS

CONTENTS

Introduction

DEVICES AND DESIRES

> Yes, I love technology, but not as much as you, you see. But I still love technology, always and forever.
>
> **Kip in *Napoleon Dynamite***

I have a love-hate relationship with technology.

Most of us are well acquainted with this feeling, but we can't quite put our finger on why. We know we're obsessed with our devices, but we don't know how to manage the challenges that come with using them, challenges that continue to multiply.

We're busy, but bored.

We're full, but empty.

We're connected, but lonelier than ever.

Our lives are filled with more activities than we thought possible, but we often feel hollow at the end of the day. We have more stuff—cars, homes, clothes, gadgets, toys—than any generation in history, yet we long for more. We're more connected online than ever, but we often feel more alone than we can describe. We know God intends for us to have something different, something better, something more. But we aren't sure how to find it.

Most everyone seems to agree that life is getting busier, crazier, and more frantic each day. We're bombarded by more information than we know how to process—news, ads, commercials, blogs, tweets, pictures, sound bites, music, games, more ads. What's crazy is that we now have more devices, programs, and apps than ever before vying to fulfill our needs. Our world abounds with countless technological breakthroughs, each one promising to make our lives better.

> We're more connected online than ever, but we often feel more alone than we can describe. Can you relate?

Unquestionably many of these innovations *have* made our lives better. I can text my close friend in Australia to let him know I'm praying for him. I can share pictures of my son's birthday party with relatives thousands of miles away. I can check my retirement fund, buy groceries, or book a hotel at the beach, all with my phone. Yet with all these upsides, I can't help but wonder about the unintended downsides of some of these conveniences that now I "can't live without."

I'm truly fascinated by how technology and social media impact our lives, our relationships, and even our faith. I don't know about you, but I have to admit I'm conflicted. I passionately love technology, using it almost nonstop every day of my life. At the same time, I absolutely can't stand it. I hate that I'm consumed with it, dependent on it, and sometimes almost unable to stop my compulsion to run to it as if it holds the answer to everything important in my life.

#CHANGEISCONSTANT

Think about how quickly the world has changed during our lifetimes. I remember when cell phones first became affordable. I wondered why anyone would want one. Sure, they sounded great if you were a doctor or on call 24/7, but I recall thinking what a burden having one would be. People could reach me at any time.

I would *never* want that.

How things have changed. Instead of not wanting a mobile phone, I almost have a panic attack if I ever leave my phone at home or the office. This may sound crazy to you (or you may know *exactly* what I'm talking about), but I don't even like leaving my phone in another room of the house when I'm home. I might miss an important call from my dentist reminding me of my next appointment or someone asking me to dedicate their new kitten to the Lord. (The answer is no.) Or a text might pop up from one of my kids upstairs wondering what's for dinner—yeah, you know, *urgent.*

I've reached a point where I *have* to have my phone nearby.

It's sick, I know.

A tool I initially avoided has become a lifeline.

Email is another story. I can remember in 1997 getting my first email account, a free one on Juno. (Believe it or not, that first email address is still active; it's where I send everything I never want to see.) At first I wasn't sure email was for me. Sure, I could see why some people might need it for business, but I didn't have anyone I needed to talk to from computer to computer. Who does that? And why couldn't you just pick up a phone and call them? So much easier and quicker, right? You probably guessed it. Within a year I was wondering how anyone ever survived without email.

I didn't think I needed it. Then I felt I couldn't live without it.

Before long, I felt like a prisoner to it.

Thankfully, email doesn't seem to be as big (at least with my friends and colleagues) as it used to be. Now anyone I really want to hear from can reach me directly by text. I still depend on email, but I don't really like it. I always feel like I'm never caught up, and when I don't check it for more than a couple of hours on a workday, I worry about who might be awaiting some response from me.

But I can't deny the many ways technology has made our lives so much easier.

We used to have to drive to a mall to shop for clothes. I haven't done that in years. Now it's *click, click, click,* and I just bought a pair of jeans, a shirt, and some new kicks. Same with the bank. No need to drive up to the window when I can bank online.

And my smart phone takes this to a whole other level. It can log how many calories I've eaten and how many steps I've taken. It can tell me the weather forecast in Bangladesh or in Paris, show me where my twenty-year-old daughter's car is, read the Bible to me, and make an egg-salad sandwich. (Okay, it can't do that last thing. At least not yet.)

It's undeniable that technology improves our lives. The same is true of social media. Facebook, Twitter, Instagram, Snapchat, LinkedIn, Vine, Pinterest, Tumblr, NewAppJustCreatedbySomeKidinCalifornia. Our indescribably big world has become infinitely smaller. Now we can reconnect with our best friend from the second grade whom we lost track of decades ago. We can follow everything our favorite celebrities or professional athletes have to say, as long as it's 140 characters or less. And we can share duck-face selfies with all of our followers.

But have we reached a point where technology and social media can hurt us as much as they help us?

WHAT'S THE PROBLEM?

Now, before you think this is going to turn into some anti-technology, boycott-social-media book, I hope you can hear the heart behind this message. I embrace everything good that our tech age offers. We can learn about virtually anything we want to. We can connect with people all over the world. And we can share our thoughts, ideas, and feelings on every subject, with everyone, anytime we want. I love what we can do with technology.

As a pastor, I also love that we can use technology to reach people with the good news of the gospel in mind-blowing ways. Most people assume the last great innovation with the Bible took place in 1455 when Gutenberg invented the printing press. But mobile devices can share more copies of God's Word now than Gutenberg ever imagined.

Our church, LifeChurch.tv, started the YouVersion Bible App back in 2008. As of today, more than 200 million people have downloaded the app for free on their mobile devices. By the grace of God, as of this moment, more than four million people are downloading the app each month. Because of the generosity of publishers and translators, our Bible App has more than a thousand versions supported in more than seven hundred languages and thousands of Bible reading plans to choose from. And if you're not a reader, that's no problem. The Bible App can even read Scripture to you.

If you are under the age of twenty-five, our ever-clicking world is, for the most part, all you've really known. You've never had to pay extra for long-distance phone calls, let alone put a quarter into a pay phone. You probably don't know most of the phone numbers you use every day because they've always been stored in your mobile device. Cassette tapes, let alone eight-track tapes, are historical artifacts. Chances are good that you might not even know what a pager is—which is something you can thank God for!

But those around my age, forty and over, remember when you had to answer your landline phone (you do remember those, right?) without knowing who was calling. And if you tried to call someone who was already on the phone, you got a busy signal and had to try again later. If they weren't home, you couldn't leave a voice mail message. Can you imagine? How did we ever communicate?

Movies you could watch only in theaters, or years later when they made it to TV. And you had to sit by the TV to watch them. If you got up to go to the bathroom, you'd miss part of the show. We purchased music in either a vinyl or plastic form and played it on special devices now found in retro thrift stores across the nation. Computers took up half a room and were only for scientists, engineers, and accountants.

Ah, the good old days.

We had plenty of struggles and distractions back then too, as people have had throughout history. But there's something different about what we're experiencing now. Some of us are starting to sense that something is wrong, even if we can't identify what it is. We still have the age-old struggles with comparison, envy, jealousy, greed, lust, and a variety of addictions. Only now we have new ways to escape from those "real life" struggles even as we create new battles in the virtual worlds we inhabit. This combination is what I call #struggles.

> **Some of us are starting to sense that something is wrong, even if we can't identify what it is.**

While I can't speak for you, I'm finally willing to admit the truth. I'm tethered to my phone, addicted to my favorite apps, and hooked on social media. Technology has become central to my life. I don't really control it. It controls me. And I don't like that.

FOR BETTER OR WORSE

Intuitively, we know that technology and social media are changing us. For better or worse, they are changing how we receive information, how we relate to people, how we see ourselves, and possibly what we value and believe about God.

Without a doubt, technology is changing the way we relate to people. While technology comes with many benefits, it also has drawbacks. The term *friend* has evolved to even mean someone you've never met but who has access to your social media online. As a result, we can define friendship on our own terms based on who we follow, "Friend," or "Like." We're becoming addicted to immediate gratification even as we attempt to control how others perceive us by what we post, pin, and tweet. Real-life, unscripted communication frightens many people now, especially young adults who are used to editing their emails, texts, and captions.

Recent studies indicate we're more connected online, but less compassionate about real people's needs. We're becoming more isolated as the depth of our relationships decreases. We crave the approval of others, their attention and affirmation, but we avoid sharing about our lives below the surface. These are just a few of the issues we'll explore in this book.

REGAINING #CONTROL

With these #struggles in mind, we will look at eight biblical values and how they can help us restore balance in our lives and end our unhealthy over-reliance on technology.

- *Contentment:* The more we compare, the less satisfied we are. Studies show that viewing social media often leaves us feeling depressed.
- *Intimacy:* The more we interact online, the more we crave face-to-face intimacy, but the more elusive it becomes.

- *Authenticity:* The more filtered our lives become, the harder it is for us to be genuine and transparent.

- *Compassion:* The more pain we're exposed to, the more difficult it is for us to care. We become desensitized to the suffering of people around us and around the world.

- *Integrity:* We're tempted nonstop to see things that pollute the purity God desires.

- *Encouragement:* Constant online criticism encourages us to focus on the weaknesses, flaws, and failures of others instead of encouraging them.

Even if you've never tweeted, posted, uploaded, or commented, you still live in a selfie-centered world. And in your heart, you know there's more than what you see.

- *Worship:* God wants to be first in our lives, but people are finding it increasingly difficult to follow Jesus in a selfie-centered world. It's time to tear all idols down.

- *Rest:* We have the world at our fingertips, and it's overwhelmingly exciting. But we need to rediscover rest and solitude.

Even if you're not a regular user of social media, or if you already have technology under control, this book can still speak to you because we all battle spiritual distractions, discontent, and temptations. Even if you've never tweeted, posted, uploaded, or commented, you still live in a selfie-centered world. And in your heart, you know there's more than what you see.

You love technology and all it offers. But you also hate it.

I can't prove this, but I have some theories, which I'll be sharing, about why we hate social media. In a nutshell, it makes everything so much about us. We're sucked into measuring our lives by how many followers we have and who they are. We want to believe we're not the sum of the Likes our last post received, but it still feels like those little clicks matter. The odd thing is the more we focus on our selves, the less satisfied we feel. And the more we're consumed with the things of this earth, the more we feel empty.

The reason is that we were created for more—much more. We were created not for earth but for eternity. We were created not to be Liked but to show love. We were created not to draw attention to ourselves but to give glory to God. We were created not to collect followers but to follow Christ.

I'm writing this book because it's time to be honest about our #struggles and to regain control of the amazing tools that technology provides us.

It's time to put technology back in its place.

It's time to love God with our whole hearts.

Chapter 1

RECOVERING CONTENTMENT

The Struggle with Comparisons

Contentment is the only real wealth.

Alfred Nobel

I used to think I had a lot of friends. You know, friends at work, friends at church, friends in the neighborhood. We'd grab lunch or talk at our kids' soccer practice, after church on Sunday or when we were out working in the yard. Then after Facebook, I was able to connect with long-distance friends and people I knew from high school and college. But everyone's so busy now. I supposedly have over three hundred friends on all my pages and sites. But last week I couldn't find one friend who could meet me for coffee. I've never felt so lonely in my entire life.

Carla S.

My buddy Steve is the most competitive guy I know. He not only has to one-up anything I say or do, but then he has to tweet about it. And post a selfie with whatever award he won, with the new jacket he got, or the cool place he just visited. I used to feel really good about my life and what I've been able to achieve. But I look at Steve and feel like I can never catch up. I would never tell him—or anyone I know—this, but it makes me feel like a loser, like I'm no good at anything.

John K.

I guess you could say I have a perpetual case of buyer's remorse. Whenever I'm about to buy something, especially if it's a big purchase, I like to research it online, you know, reading customer reviews and consumer reports from the experts. Then I'll shop around and try to find the best price before I finally enter my credit card and hit "buy now." But when I get the item a few days later, I'll wish I had ordered something else. Sometimes I send it back only to start the whole process over again. It doesn't seem to matter if it's a new sweater, a food processor, something for the kids, or throw pillows for the couch. Nothing ever seems to be as good as I hoped it would be.

Sarah W.

1.1 I WANT THE FONZ

I remember the first time I was crushed by comparisons.

I was in junior high in Beaumont, Texas, and once—for about a week—I was the king of the world. I was the first kid at Marshall Middle School to get a motorized vehicle of any kind. Scooters are much more common today, but that's not the kind of machine I'm talking about. To call my fire-red moped a scooter would be very generous. I had the kind of moped that I like to think of as "the original": it was essentially a bicycle with a motor. And that motor had a governor that wouldn't let the bike go more than twenty-five miles an hour, even downhill, but I'd imagine I was going fifty. Unfortunately, my moped didn't always have enough power to go uphill, either. It had pedals so you could add your own power to help it along.

When I rode my moped, especially on level streets, I imagined that I looked pretty cool, like one of the Sons of Anarchy on a huge Harley. In reality, especially pedaling as hard as I could uphill, I probably looked more like Nacho Libre. But whatever I looked like didn't matter, because Tiffany, a girl who lived around the corner from me, thought my moped was the coolest thing ever. I'd strap on my blue helmet (which of course matched my moped) and buzz around the corner and four blocks over to Tiffany's house to pick her up. Tiffany would hop on behind me, wrap her arms around my waist, and we'd go zipping off, probably twenty miles an hour given the added weight, her hair flying behind us. Life was good.

Until Brian Marquardt got a motorcycle.

I buzzed over to Tiffany's house, parked my sweet ride out front, and strutted up to ring her doorbell. When Tiffany answered the door, she kind of frowned at me. "Oh," she said. "It's you. I'm not riding with you today."

"Why not?" I asked.

Tiffany held one of her hands out in front of her and examined her perfect fingernails as she spoke. "Because," she said, "I'm riding with Brian."

I struggled to process this new information. "But I thought we . . . I mean . . . I have my helmet here and everything . . . and your hair is so pretty . . . and it flies out behind you . . . and . . ."

But despite the airtight case I was making, Tiffany looked at me like she felt sad for me or something, shook her head slightly, and said simply, "No."

I just stood there awkwardly for what seemed like several minutes. "Brian Marquardt? Really?"

She looked at me dismissively and said, "Listen, I'm sorry, but you're . . . well, you're Richie Cunningham. I want the Fonz."

#HurtsSoBad.

If you don't know who Richie Cunningham or the Fonz are, #DontWorryItsOkay. I trust you can tell the difference even if you've never seen an episode of *Happy Days*. Even after all these years, I still think about that moment sometimes, which shows you how far we go with making comparisons. My view of who I was didn't match up with what Tiffany saw, and I was crushed. I couldn't believe I didn't measure up to someone else. I was not good enough. That experience still has the potential to hurt me, even though I'm married to a wonderful woman and we are incredibly blessed.

And I know I'm not the only one who has experienced this hurt.

Recently at one of my son's soccer games, I overheard two moms telling each other they were jealous of the things they saw each other post on social media. One mom has a full-time job, and she told her stay-at-home friend how much she envied her. "Every time I see something you've pinned on Pinterest, I just feel ashamed. You pour so much into your kids. They're always smiling and happy. And when I see all the activities you do with them, all those cute crafts and delicious homemade foods, I just feel like a big failure as a mom."

The stay-at-home mom laughed. "Are you kidding me? You have no idea how jealous I am of *you!* Every day I see you getting to do all kinds of interesting things—constantly checking into new places, meeting new people. And you have the best wardrobe—I just love your shoes! Seriously, I'm lucky if I change out of my pajamas before noon. Sure, I love my kids, but I feel like I constantly have to come up with new things for them to do to keep them from driving me crazy. You know, 'Mom, we're bored!'"

Both moms are living great lives.

But they're jealous of the things others have that they don't have.

If you're on social media, you know exactly what I'm talking about.

You're sitting on your couch in your old sweats, enjoying a plate of mac and cheese and an apple on your lap, flipping through your phone, when you see a friend instagram the *amazing* dinner she's having on yet another date. The candlelight glows beautifully and her hair looks perfect, and is that another new designer dress? The linen tablecloth is so white it almost sparkles, and the place setting looks so elegant. It's clearly a nice restaurant overlooking the city. Her picture even has a frame—and how did she get two hundred Likes in less than an hour?

Or your buddy posts a selfie from the free-weight room at the gym, lifting his shirt to make sure you can see his ripped abs in the mirror. He's ready for the *300* sequel while you, well, you're at home single-handedly trying to eat Hostess out of bankruptcy.

Know what I'm talking about?

Another thing technology lets us do is measure our popularity, often with painful accuracy. Back when I was a kid, you had to estimate how unpopular you were: "Let's see . . . No one will sit with me in the cafeteria. So far, I've asked three different girls to the Valentine's dance and gotten three firm no's. I lost the election to be hall monitor—again. Hmm . . . I guess I must not be very popular."

Now empirical data can tell you with absolute precision where you rank: "Let's see . . . If I have seventy-three followers, and my BFF has 423, that means she's almost six times more popular than I am. My last three pics got twenty-nine, thirty-three, and eighteen Likes. Her last three got eighty-eight and seventy-three—then she hit triple digits with that stupid puppy pic. #MyLifeSucks."

It's arguable that no generation before us has struggled with discontent as much as ours. Although we still have poverty and economic inequality, the everyday lives of most of us are filled with convenience, opportunity, and abundance—sometimes to the point of excess. Yet it doesn't take much for us to feel as though we aren't getting everything we deserve and to face disappointment. Add social media and what do you get? Never before have so many people had so much and felt so dissatisfied.

Some sociologists point to technology as a significant factor in our constant unhappiness. We are the first people in the history of the world who are able to see inside the lives of others in real time. We carry tiny media powerhouses in our pockets that enable us to follow other people's lives through their check-ins, pictures, and videos.

And if what we're seeing in the lives of others seems better, more interesting, and more fulfilling than our own lives, we feel like we're missing out. Of course, that feed we're watching may not reflect reality. Most people put their best foot forward, showing only the things they want others to see. As my close friend and fellow pastor Steven Furtick explains, "We compare our behind-the-scenes with other people's highlight reels." Photoshopped and cropped, filtered and edited, what we see online makes our own reality seem dingy and dull.

Never before have so many people had so much and felt so dissatisfied.

No wonder we often feel so dissatisfied.

No matter how much we have, it can't compare to what others appear to have.

1.2 #GETREAL

This dissatisfaction isn't just something that only I deal with. A recent study sought to quantify how exposure to social media affects people's moods. Researchers at two universities tracked students who were regular Facebook users over two weeks by having them complete life-satisfaction surveys five times a day.[1] After students spent time on Facebook, their surveys showed them to be considerably less satisfied and more critical of their own lives than they were before the Facebook time. Results also indicated that more than one third of the test subjects felt "significantly worse" about themselves the more time they spent on Facebook. Why? We aren't designed by God to seek the image of others; we are designed to seek him. When we spend time on social media focusing on how well others present their lives, we are, to use one of my father's baseball analogies, taking our eye off the ball.

Since this is a very real issue for many of us, I'd like to give you a chance to #GetReal with me. Let's take a few minutes to expose any discontent—which is another way of saying envy—that you might be harboring in your heart. We'll look at three categories, and I want you to be gut-level honest if you see yourself in any of them.

First, do you battle with material and *financial envy?* Here's how you can tell if you do: when a friend tweets about their new car, do you immediately picture your piece-of-junk car that barely starts? Or let's say someone from work posts a picture from the beach. Is your first thought, "Wait . . . isn't this their second beach trip already this year?" (But who's counting, right?) Or let's say your friend posts another #OOTD (outfit of the day), and you start scrolling through her posts, and it dawns on you—this girl owns more kinds of shoes than Zappos carries? Be honest: do you battle with material and financial discontent?

Second, do you harbor *relational envy?* When all your friends' photos from their dinner out together start showing up in your feed—all at the same time—do you wonder, "How come no one invited me?" Maybe you're not in a relationship, and you want to be, and it's springtime, and it seems like everyone you know is getting married. Part of you wants to be happy for your friends because you love them. But if you're honest, it also kind of hurts to see them all pairing off and smiling with their new spouses. Do you feel left out, overlooked, unwanted?

It could be you're working two jobs, exhausted with struggling to keep your head above water and feeling sad that you can't give your kids as much time and attention as you want to. And you have that one friend who always seems to be with their kids at the game, or taking them to the lake or to the amusement park (again), or even just doing simple things like reading to them at bedtime. Instead of feeling happy for your friend, do you feel guilty about all the things you can't do with your kids? If you respond in any of these ways, let's call your attitude what it is: relational envy.

Finally, maybe you battle with *circumstantial envy*. You see what other people are doing, where they're working, how they're living. Do you then look at your life, your circumstances, and wonder why you don't have the things they have or get to do the things they're doing? Do you think to yourself, "I really thought by this age I'd be more successful—or at least doing something I enjoy"?

Perhaps you want to have a baby, but you don't see that happening anytime soon. Then it seems like every time you look at your feed, you see someone else posting collages of their pregnancy months or their "gender reveal party." Do you think, "Well, yippedeedoo! Their cake was pink inside!"? If you do, you're probably green with envy.

1.3 ACHIEVE, CONQUER, ACCUMULATE

If I'm honest, circumstantial envy is harder for me than the other two (financial and relational). Since I'm a pastor, I work weekends, both Saturday and Sunday. So when I'm "on," most of my friends and church members are "off." I can barely look at social media on the weekends because all I see are people at football games, or playing Frisbee, or riding bikes, or jumping waves on Sea-Doos. It makes me crazy jealous. I just have to tell myself, "Well, I guess I'll just save the world for the glory of God while everyone else is out having fun doing all that stupid stuff." But the truth is, telling myself that doesn't make me feel any better.

Chuck Swindoll is credited with saying, "Life is 10 percent what happens to you and 90 percent how you respond." Of course, most of us probably feel like life is exactly the opposite. We live as though it's 90 percent (or more) what happens to us. And sometimes we feel like our response doesn't make any difference at all.

I can't think of anyone in history who had a better understanding of managing his responses than the apostle Paul. When he was in a prison in Rome, chained twenty-four hours a day to a guard (they took shifts), Paul wrote these words: "I know what it is to be in need, and I know what it is to have plenty. I have learned the secret of being content in any and every situation, whether well fed or hungry, whether living in plenty or in want. I can do all this through [Christ] who gives me strength" (Phil. 4:12–13).

Let's break that statement down. Paul is essentially saying, "I've gone without the things that I need before. But I've also had times when I had more than enough. Life happens in seasons. I've had good seasons when everything was going well, and I've had hard ones when nothing went my way. But in all of that living, I've learned that there's one secret to being content, no matter what my circumstances happen to be at the time. And that secret is that I can do anything and everything not by my power but through Christ. He's the one who gives me the strength to handle anything that comes my way."

> You will battle with discontent until you let Christ be all that you need.

Don't miss this truth. You will battle with discontent until you let Christ be all that you need. Don't believe me? Then prove me wrong. Chase after everything you've ever wanted. Go ahead. I dare you. I double-dog dare you. Go earn as much money as you can.

Buy whatever you want. Achieve, conquer, accumulate, repeat. Sound familiar? Maybe you've already tried some of these things, or at least known someone else who has. None of it works.

At the end of the day, every day, you'll still feel empty.

1.4 ALL YOU NEED

Maybe you're not really into material things. Maybe the party scene is more your thing. Then try that. Go party your brains out. Seek every thrill, pursue every high, get every buzz you can find. Guess what? When the party's over and everyone's gone home and that killer hangover finally starts to fade, there you'll be, right back where you started, still longing for more.

Maybe you're more of a people person. You just haven't found the right person who meets all your needs. So keep trying. Find a new boyfriend or girlfriend. If that person doesn't work out, try another. If someone else still doesn't scratch your itch, maybe just one person isn't enough. Trade out all of your old friends for new ones. Get popular. (Lots of books and websites promise to teach you how.) Who knows? Maybe you can even become famous! But after everybody leaves and the lights go down, it'll be just you again, alone, still lonely, still longing.

If you're going to try any or all of these things, be sure you capture every moment. Get the biggest data plan you can and collect Wi-Fi passwords at every stop. Check in at all the cool places. Share every inspirational thought you have, and every joke. Post lots of photos and videos too, of course. Never stop sharing the show as you go. Post everything online for the whole world to see. Pile up Likes and Friends and followers until it's all just one frenzied blur. Hustle until your real life exceeds your dreams. And even when you've reached the summit, I can guarantee you one thing: your longing for more will *never* stop.

Why not? Because you were created for eternity, not for this world as we know it. Nothing on earth can ever satisfy the spiritual longing you feel inside, even if you could collect it all.

Nothing.

I remember when I was a teenager, years before I knew Christ, hearing people say, "God makes a Christ-shaped void inside every person." That saying annoyed me. I did not understand what they were talking about. But then one day I learned for myself why they said it: because it is absolutely true. Nothing outside of a living relationship with Christ can ever fill the emptiness inside.

You know you've been searching. I'm here to tell you that Christ is what you're searching for. He is your source. He is your strength. He is your sustainer. He is your joy. He is your contentment. He is your all in all.

When Christ is all you have, you'll finally realize that Christ is all you need.

He's everything that matters.

> **When Christ is all you have, you'll finally realize that Christ is all you need.**

If you keep searching, comparing, and envying, you'll never have enough. So let's look at three ways we can help ourselves battle the sin of envying, keeping in mind that we'll need Christ's strength to win the war.

1.5 BEYOND COMPARE

How can we overcome the strong human drive to compare? Let's look at the first way to combat envy by turning to the Bible: "We do not dare to classify or compare ourselves with some who commend themselves. When they measure themselves by themselves and compare themselves with themselves, they are not wise" (2 Cor. 10:12).

Pastor Andy Stanley puts this more simply than anyone I know: "There is no win in comparisons." We need to kill our comparisons because they are more serious than most of us realize. Let's look at another passage, and hopefully you'll see what I mean: "But if you harbor bitter envy and selfish ambition in your hearts, do not boast about it or deny the truth. Such 'wisdom' does not come down from heaven but is earthly, unspiritual, demonic. For where you have envy and selfish ambition, there you find disorder and every evil practice" (James 3:14–16).

Notice that *wisdom* is in quotes because James was being sarcastic; these attitudes are not wise. But also notice this: envy is demonic. Where envy is, there is disorder. Where envy is, there is *every* evil practice. Look at these words. Demonic? Every evil practice? This is serious. Envy is not from heaven. It's earthly. It's unspiritual. It's demonic. I don't want to participate in activities that the Bible calls demonic. I'm sure you don't either. And James doesn't say, "Probably it would be a good idea if you considered being careful about envy." He says that with envy there is evil.

> Envy is not from heaven. It's earthly. It's unspiritual. It's demonic.

Still not convinced? What about the Ten Commandments? You know, God's Top Ten that includes "You shall not covet" (Ex. 20:17)? Not your neighbors' house. Not your friend's spouse. Not your coworker's car. Nothing and no one belonging to someone else. Not even their cat. (Well, now I'm putting my own interpretation on the Bible. It doesn't say anything bad about cats.)

Envy isn't just unhealthy. In God's eyes, it's downright sinful. We need to kill our comparisons, because comparing ourselves with others is not wise.

Killing comparisons looks different in different people's lives. How can you be more honest with yourself about the things that push your envy button? Maybe it's time to take a break from social media, especially if it's feeding the sin of envy in your life. I'm not saying you have to throw your phone away or cancel Wi-Fi at home. But at the very least, if you notice that you respond with envy to certain people's posts, you should hide them from your feed. Let me be clear: I believe it's best to just avoid the envy button completely. We'll talk more about unplugging in chapter 8 when we consider the topic of rest.

But if you're not willing to unplug for a while to combat envy, let me offer some other suggestions and take this discussion beyond social media. When you start flipping through the latest catalog that comes into your home, do you find yourself always wanting something more? You may need to cancel or just throw out those beautiful catalogs. Or how many shopping apps do you have on your phone? Are you addicted? Maybe you should delete those. You might need to stop watching HGTV if you just can't help sinning every time a show tours someone's palatial home while you watch from your pathetic little apartment.

Maybe you need to stop going to the boat show, or the car show, or the hunting show, or whatever show that's causing you to spend more time than you know you should wishing for something you don't have. It's time to kill comparisons and use that time for something else.

Maybe you need to stop looking at certain friends' Facebook posts because you tend to end up feeling jealous, envious, or covetous, or inadequate, unsatisfied, and generally discontent with your life when you see all that they appear to have. Why? Because envy is a wildfire, always consuming and never quenched. It's demonic. It causes "every evil practice" to lurk inside you, including lust, that longing for something more that is insatiable.

The first step in combatting envy is to consider what you can and should give up. Just choose one thing to *stop* doing today. For example, stop checking your Facebook feed before bed. Don't post a picture of the delicious plate of food you've been served at a restaurant. Stop reciprocating with everyone who follows you on LinkedIn, especially if you don't know them. Practice stopping that behavior over and over. Ask others around you to help you stop. Commit to yourself and to them that you will stop. The next step will show you how you can help yourself stop, which will make your commitment easier to keep.

1.6 SHOT TO THE HEART

Killing comparisons doesn't mean just identifying the bad influences in your life and cleaning them out. The second practical thing you can do to kill comparisons is to celebrate other people's successes. When you see someone else being blessed in a way that you hope to be blessed, celebrating with them can purify the intentions of your heart.

Did someone else get the job you wanted? Try this prayer: "God, you must have had a reason to bless them. Thank you, Father, for your blessings in that person's life." When you see someone else get that thing you've always wanted, try thanking God instead of wallowing in jealousy: "God, thank you so much that your hand of blessing is on them. Please continue blessing them." Celebration sends a kill shot right to the heart of envy.

I wrote this book during a very busy season in my life. I was really looking forward to the next opportunity for my family to take a vacation, and I started seeing pictures online from a couple I know who were traveling overseas. Dublin, Ireland. Edinburgh, Scotland. Topped off by snowmobiling. Across a glacier. In Iceland. And this was all on the same trip! "Thank you, Father, that they're having such a great time," I prayed. "This trip is such a big blessing to them." Suffocate the flames of envy with a blanket of gratitude.

Not celebrating the blessings of others also affects how God works through our lives. Back here in my normal, everyday life, I'm convinced that when I can't cele-

> **Celebration sends a kill shot right to the heart of envy.**

brate for others, I actually limit what God wants to do through me. Our church is almost twenty years old. Throughout those years, we've been blessed with seeing the number of people we're able to reach expand—except for two seasons. When I look back on those periods when we weren't growing, I recognize that both times I was carrying significant sin in my heart.

Not only were we not reaching new people in one of those seasons, we were actually losing people. At the time, our church had two locations, and on Sundays I used to drive back and forth between them to preach. On that drive, I passed a small church. It was obviously struggling and had only eight to ten cars in the parking lot each week. I would pray for them sometimes, something like, "Father, bless this little church. Please help them find their stride." But to be honest, even as I was praying that with my lips, in my heart I felt proud. I was thinking, "Whew! I'm sure glad our church isn't going through that." It was a sick kind of pride that involved carefully counting their cars every time I passed by.

This isn't the sort of thing I say often, but I really believe God spoke to me. Now, just to be clear, I'm not saying I heard the audible voice of God booming in my car. But I can honestly say that I felt a sort of presence, a power that filled my car, and I clearly heard these words inside my head spoken by a voice that wasn't my own: "Would you really be happy if I blessed them? And if I blessed them more than I am blessing you?"

I realized that my honest answers to those questions would not honor God. "Nope. That would not really make me happy. Bless them a lot, God. Just please don't bless them as much as you're blessing our church." I felt sick in the pit of my stomach when I saw that my heart was impure. My heart wasn't about building God's kingdom; it was more about building my own kingdom. And that is a very dangerous place for a pastor to be.

I started praying about it right then and turned it over and over in my mind for several days. Then I repented sincerely. I cried out, "God, I really want to come to a place where I want you to bless other churches more than you're blessing ours." God honored that prayer and changed my heart so that my life became completely about his kingdom again, and then he blessed our church again with growth.

The next thing I'm going to say, I can't prove. It's not in the Bible, so take it with a grain of salt. But in my heart, I live this as if it's true: perhaps the reason God is not blessing you with something you want is because you're not celebrating God's blessings in someone else's life. Just as I don't want to take God's blessings in my life for granted, I want to always celebrate his blessings in the lives of others, because we're told to "rejoice with those who rejoice" (Rom. 12:15). I don't want my life to be about me. Jesus calls us to something better, something higher.

1.7 A CONTINUAL FEAST

A third way to kill comparisons is to cultivate gratitude. I read an excellent definition of envy that went something like this: envy is resenting God's goodness in other people's lives and ignoring God's goodness in your own life. That's powerful stuff.

Speaking of powerful, here's another verse on this topic that I just love: Proverbs 15:15 says, "For the despondent, every day brings trouble" (NLT). All of us know someone like this. (You might even be a bit like this.)

- "Man, I can just tell today's gonna be a bad day."
- "Well, isn't that just great! It's going to rain all day tomorrow."
- "Just checked the markets. The economy's in the toilet for sure."
- "My kids are always so difficult. Every day it's the same thing."
- "I sure do hate this car. It's going to give out any day now. I can feel it."

The despondent see every single day bringing more trouble. They can't see the blessings because their glass is always half-empty.

But Proverbs 15:15 doesn't end there. That's only the first half. The second half says, "For the happy heart, life is a continual feast" (NLT).

Are people who start the day miserable living in the same day as people with a happy heart? Of course they are! The difference is in what they're looking for. Despondent people are looking for trouble—and they find it. People with a happy heart are looking for God's goodness—and they find it!

If you want to look for the bad in this world, you will certainly find plenty. Trouble's not hard to find. But have you considered looking for the good? There is just as much of it, if not more. If you'll just look for the blessings of God, you'll find them!

"For the happy heart, life is a continual feast."

Despondent people are looking for trouble—and they find it. People with a happy heart are looking for God's goodness—and they find it!

Every time I read this verse, I am reminded of my dad. Of all the things I admire about my dad—and there are a lot—the thing I admire most is his positive perspective on life. Every time I call my dad, he says the same thing.

"Hey, Dad, how's it going?"

"Son, life is good!"

This is another of those things that, when I was younger, used to kind of annoy me. My dad said this so often, I thought it was automatic, just something he said.

I remember when he was battling to recover from a serious stroke that could have taken his life. Very concerned, I asked him, "Hey, Dad, how you doing?"

Without missing a beat, he answered, "Oh . . . (*cough, cough*) life is good."

"It doesn't sound good, Dad!"

"What? No, it *is* good."

One day I finally asked him about it. I said, "Dad, do you realize that you always say, 'Life is good,' no matter what's going on? No matter how you're really doing?"

A funny thing about my dad is that he loves to communicate in baseball terms. For example, if I'm preaching, he says I'm "on the mound." Then instead of saying, "Preach well," he says, "Keep 'em low and inside." When I was surprised that he was so positive even though he had significant stroke-related issues, he said, "Well, Craig, I say that life is good because it's true. Son, you know I could have died. The way I see it, I'm living in extra innings right now. It's true. Life is good."

I love that! My dad says "life is good" because he genuinely believes it is, no matter what. It's in his heart. And he's right!

It's all about perspective.

"For the happy heart, life is a continual feast."

Some people believe that Solomon wasn't just the richest man of his time but that accounting for things like inflation, resource distribution, and population density, Solomon was the richest man of all time. That guy said this: "Enjoy what you have rather than desiring what you don't have" (Eccl. 6:9 NLT).

You want to have a nonstop party? Enjoy what God has given you, instead of longing for what you don't have. Be thankful for what God has given you, instead of resenting other peoples' instagrams: "Oh, I wish I had their life!" Guess what? They're longing for your life in ways you don't even know about!

The next time you feel tempted to say, "I hate my stupid car," try praying instead, "Thank you, Lord, that I have a car that runs. I'm grateful that I'm blessed to be in the 8 percent of all people in the world who own a car. Thank you, God, for my wonderful car!"

When you are tempted to say, "I wish I had a bigger house," try praying this instead: "Thank you, Lord, that I have a roof over my head—and indoor plumbing that works!" Do you realize that half of the people in the world don't have that? Clean, running water inside their house? That's amazing! It's a significant blessing from God, and we should and can be grateful to have it.

Are you tempted to complain, "My life is so crazy right now. I'm just so busy"? Why is your life so busy? Because you have a family? Because you have children? Because your healthy children are involved in activities? With friends they enjoy? Because you have a thriving community that you're contributing to? Try praying instead, "Thank you, God, that I have so many opportunities to bless other people. Thank you for giving my life significance. I'm so grateful that you have given me so many people in my life that I care about."

With Christ's help, let's kill comparisons. Envy is earthly and unspiritual. It's demonic. Every evil practice is bound up in envy. Instead, let's celebrate the blessings God gives to others. Social media should be a place to see what's happening in the lives of those you love, not a place that makes you envious. Let's rejoice with those who rejoice. Let's cultivate gratitude.

Let's worship our God not because he gives us everything we want but because he is worthy of our praise. Let's worship him because we've learned the secret of being content, whether we're living in plenty or living in want. That secret is that we can do all things through the Son of God, Jesus Christ, who gives us strength.

Because Jesus is all we need, let's pursue him with our whole hearts.

Only in him will we find true joy and true contentment.

Only he is life, and only he truly satisfies.

Chapter 2

RESTORING INTIMACY

The Struggle with "Likes"

My friends tell me I have an intimacy problem. But they don't really know me.

Garry Shandling

After graduating, I thought I'd stay a lot closer to my friends. The good thing is that I can still see what's going on in their lives through social media. Every day I get the latest updates. Jennifer just had her second baby girl and named her Chloe. Holly finally graduated from law school after six years. And Katie and her husband just got back from the Bahamas. But even though I know all this about them, I don't feel close to them anymore. Besides a brief "hello" at Jenn's baby shower, I can't remember the last time I actually talked to one of them. Now our big reunion is in two weeks, and I'm not even sure if I want to go. What would we talk about? I'm afraid it would feel too awkward.

Michelle P.

Real relationships move too slowly for me, and face-to-face communication feels so awkward. That's why I don't date much anymore. Maybe I'm spoiled because of how quickly I can communicate with people online and on my phone. When I'm texting or chatting with someone, I can get an instant response without having to pretend to be polite or patient. If a guy doesn't respond to my text right away, then I know he's not really interested. I'm also able to have more control over the conversation, only telling someone what I want them to know. Neither of us is distracted by our body language or saying more than we intended. But I do miss the spontaneous moments when you're with someone—that and the ability to receive a hug or hold someone's hand.

Jenny K.

Maybe it's just because I'm a competitive guy, but I really start to feel down if I don't get at least a hundred Likes when I post a photo to Instagram or a status change on Facebook. I've always wanted people to like me. So for some reason I'm completely obsessed with getting people to approve of what I say or post online. But even I can acknowledge that it really doesn't matter much. So what if my college roommate likes the picture of me and my wife at dinner celebrating our anniversary? I shouldn't care, but I do. In fact, I probably spent more time trying to get the right shot to post than I did actually talking with my wife.

Tom M.

2.1 #STAYCONNECTED

"I'm really proud of you."

Just five little words. That's all it took to #MeltDadsHeart. My twenty-one-year-old daughter, Catie, had texted me at 8:22 p.m. on Sunday night not long ago. (I know 'cause I saved it.) It was one of those special moments when she surprised me with the simple gift of those five little words. It meant even more to me because now that Catie is an adult and out on her own, it was totally unexpected. The fact that she was thinking of me, and was *proud* of me, means more to me than she could ever know.

One quick text is all it took for me to feel #SoHappy #LoveThatGirl #LifeIsGreat.

There's no denying it. Technology helps us communicate in so many as-tounding ways—across the country, around the world, any time, day or night. You've probably had your own special moments like I had with Catie, times when a sweet text, a funny selfie, or an unexpected FaceTime call lifted your spirits.

You've probably also seen the way Apple, Samsung, Microsoft, and every other tech company capitalize on the ways their products keep us connect-ed with friends and family. You know, those commercials with grandparents talking to their grandkids on video chat through a tablet. Or a mom or dad in the military skyping in Christmas morning. One commercial shows a healthy newborn baby in a hospital room being watched by anxious family members in another country. Another shows a dad who's away on a business trip reading a bedtime story to his little boy at home. And it's the weirdest thing: every time I see that one, something gets in my eye and it starts watering. So odd.

Maybe a particular ad touches some soft spot in you, one that hits close to home and makes you appreciate the benefits of our ability to call, text, skype, chat, post, and click. But if we're honest, we all admit that while technology greatly enhances our ability to stay in touch with people in our lives, the contact is not the same as actually being together and sharing the important events.

It's one thing to FaceTime into a child's first birthday party. It's another to actually taste the cake, hold the little one, feel her breath blowing out the single candle, and hear her laughter in your ear as you hold her close. As much as tech providers and gadget companies want us to believe that we can stay connected wherever we are and whatever we're doing, it's not the same as *being there*.

Technology's impact on our ability to relate, communicate, and connect with other people includes some unintended negative consequences. If we want to be good stewards of the amazing capabilities that technology affords us, we have to navigate very carefully. Social media allows us to connect with others in so many unique and often meaningful ways. But if we spend all our time and energy online, we lose true intimacy with the people around us. While we're linked to dozens, hundreds, or even thousands of other people, we're often detaching from interpersonal relationships.

This is not always the case, of course. It really all depends on how we choose to use social media and technology in our relationships. At our church, we've seen the fruits of doing ministry through social media and other forms of technology, from sharing Scriptures and prayer requests to simply informing people of ways

> We have to make sure technology is enhancing our relationships, not replacing them.

they can make a difference. I would even go so far as to say it's okay to love technology. But we have to manage it. We have to make sure technology is enhancing our relationships, not replacing them. We need to make sure our ability to communicate doesn't cause us to talk more while actually saying less. We must focus on loving others more and truly interacting with them, rather than just Liking what they post.

2.2 WET FEET

How is technology changing your relationships?

I don't want you to miss the significance of this question. I'm serious. I want you to really think about it, not just generally as some social problem in our changing world but as something that affects *you, your* life, *your* relationships.

To help you think through this question, let me share a litmus test I use. This standard reminds me of how I aspire to love and serve those around me and of what it means to love, really love, and not just to Like. After applying this standard, I can better determine whether technology is helping or hindering how well I am loving other people.

A quiet little scene from Jesus' life turns up the volume on how we love each other. During his final Passover meal with his disciples, what we often call the Last Supper, and just before one of his closest friends and followers, Judas, betrayed him, Jesus washed his disciples' feet (see John 13:1–17).

I cannot emphasize enough how significant this act was. Just think about it: washing a person's feet was the job of a servant or slave. People of nobility and wealth had servants to perform menial tasks like this. Imagine the master coming home and calling from the front door for a servant to come and wash his feet so he wouldn't track filth from the streets into his home. The servant's position was the one Jesus chose to place himself in. Jesus—the very Son of God—washed the feet of not even nobles but twelve rowdy, dirty-footed guys.

Jesus was demonstrating his love for them and his commitment to them. He wanted to make it clear that he did not consider himself too high and mighty to do one of the most menial, most personal tasks one person can do for another. Not surprisingly, here's what Jesus said after the meal: "A new command I give you: Love one another. As I have loved you, so you must love one another. By this everyone will know that you are my disciples, if you love one another" (John 13:34–35).

It's important to consider not just what Jesus said but even what he didn't say. Notice he said that "everyone will know that you are my disciples, if you love one another."

Jesus *didn't* say "everyone will know that you are my disciples if you have perfect theology." Certainly good theology is important, but it's not how the world will be able to see that we follow Christ.

Jesus *didn't* say "everyone will know that you are my disciples if you attend church regularly." Does this mean we don't need to go to church? Of course not! We're supposed to spend time together to encourage each other in the things of God (Heb. 10:24–25). But going to church isn't what shows the world that we follow Jesus either.

The way they will know we are his disciples—according to Jesus—is how *we love one another*. He set the example for us himself by washing his disciples' feet, an act of absolute humility. We should treat one another in ways that show that the sacrificial love of Jesus lives inside our hearts. That's how the world will know that we are his disciples.

And that's how we will know if technology is in its proper place in our lives: by how well we love one another. It's hard to wash someone's feet with a phone in your hand.

So be honest with yourself as you listen for God's voice. Are you sending emails when phone calls would be more meaningful? Are you typing a quick text when a personal visit would deeply impact a loved one? Have you unintentionally neglected to use your gifts to serve others because you are hoping others' Likes will serve your need to be noticed? When was the last time you actually snail-mailed a handwritten birthday card or thank-you note instead of simply texting because it was easier?

> **That's how we will know if technology is in its proper place in our lives: by how well we love one another. It's hard to wash someone's feet with a phone in your hand.**

Jesus has something better for us. Maybe it's time to put down the device and pick up a towel to serve.

2.3 YOU'VE GOT A "FRIEND"

If I've lost you on the connection between Jesus' washing his disciples' feet and the impact technology has on our relationships, please bear with me. I think you'll better understand the significance of Christ's example if we look at three major ways technology is changing the way we relate to the people in our lives. As we explore these ways, consider how each applies to your life and how you are using technology and social media to relate to others.

1. The Term *Friend* Is Evolving

It used to be that when someone said another person was a friend, you understood exactly what they meant. A friend was someone who shared common interests or bonds, someone you enjoyed being around, someone you did life with. But it's not that simple anymore, is it? Now a friend can be someone you've never met IRL (in real life). Friends can be people who follow what you post on social media. If they follow you, but you don't follow them back, that's one kind of friend. If you follow them, but they don't follow you, that's another kind of friend. And if you both follow each other, that's yet another kind of friend.

Currently, the average American Facebook user has 338 Facebook friends.[2] But surveys indicate that the average American has only two friends they consider to be close.[3] As shocking as that statistic is, I think one is even sadder:

> We have lots of online interactivity, but that doesn't mean we have any personal intimacy.

25 percent of Americans today say they have *zero* close friends![4] The #struggles are real. Does it really matter that you have 338 Facebook friends if you have no one to share your life with? And I'm not even talking about the kind of friend who listens as you pour your heart out or share your latest struggles. Many people no longer have friends they can hang out with or who can drop by unannounced as a welcome surprise. (When was the last time you did that

to someone, or they did it to you? Doesn't it sound intimidating?) Technology supposedly saves us time, yet we seem to have even less time—at least for really relating to people. We have lots of online interactivity, but that doesn't mean we have any personal intimacy.

Friend just doesn't mean what it used to.

2. We're Addicted to Immediate Affirmation

Let's say you were at home alone back in the old days (ten years ago), and you started feeling a little lonely. What would you do? You might pick up the phone and call a friend. You might even make arrangements to get together. You might walk outside and visit with your next-door neighbor. Any of these were reasonable choices, and they were all pretty easy, right? Apparently, they just weren't easy enough.

What do we do today when we feel lonely? Text a friend, post an update, or share an old favorite picture. If we're feeling really creative, we'll surf for items to pin to Pinterest or make a new YouTube video. We might take a picture of our homemade chocolate chip cookies (gluten free, no GMO, hand-whittled, and carved from organic cocoa) and share it on Instagram. Or we might Vine a little clip about being bored.

Then there's my favorite. If we're really bored and lonely, we always have ourselves. That's right, we can snap a selfie, right there on the couch. If we're really motivated, we might even go in the bathroom and fix ourselves up a little first, then snap a selfie in the bathroom mirror. We tousle our hair, puff out our lips (duck face), and tilt our heads, snapping picture after picture, trying to get the light just right, determined to achieve the "perfect" shot. We might even go as far as to wear our trendiest clothes, find a local you-wish-you-knew-where-I-was ally, channel our inner Tyra Banks, and let the self-timer rip.

But we don't have to stop there. We can touch up the photo, tweak the lighting a little more, maybe use a filter. We are nowhere near perfect, but we can manipulate images, apps, and filters to create an image of ourselves that's perfect for the moment. And don't forget the all-important caption. Is it inspirational? Clever, but not too obviously clever? We can even add a Bible verse for extra Likes. Once all is in place—drumroll, please—we can post it. Then we can compulsively check our updates, hoping we hit the Likes jackpot.

Even if we don't hit it big, we may score some fun comments. You know, things like:

- "Lookin' good!"
- "Love that shirt! Where'd ya get it???"
- "omgosh amazing *swoons*"
- "where r u? totes adorbs!! [sexy, smiling emoji]"

We often get immediate feedback. But the problem with this kind of immediate feedback, this quick affirmation, is that it's addicting. Even when we know it's shallow, even when we don't believe the sender is sincere in their flattery, we still love receiving it. To be fair, it's not our fault. Scientists say that receiving positive affirmation like this releases dopamine, a chemical in our brains that gives us a kind of euphoric feeling, a little rush. Just like similar drugs, we can get addicted to that high.

If you don't believe me, consider the last time you posted a selfie and didn't get much response—at least in the first hour. Do you remember having an empty feeling and thoughts like these running through your mind?

- "Where is everyone? What's up with that?"
- "How many have clicked on it? Did they Like it?"
- "Who Liked it?"
- "Why didn't she Like it? She never Likes my pictures. I'm going to stop Liking hers. Just keep that up, sister, and you're gonna get yourself unfollowed."

Many of us are addicted to immediate affirmation. What is this addiction doing to us? How is it affecting our relationships?

Sociologists call all this "deferred loneliness." We're trying to meet some short-term need, but in the process of meeting this need, we're deferring a deeper, longer-term need. We are meant to have deep, sometimes difficult feelings of loneliness to motivate us toward the kinds of contact with others that meet our deeper, long-term needs. Every time we seek instant affirmation, we ignore our basic human condition of loneliness and the *opportunity of loneliness* that drives us toward real friendship, real intimacy, first with God and then with others.

We're living for Likes, but we're longing for love.

So our addiction to instant gratification can stunt our relationships.

We're living for Likes, but we're longing for love.

3. We Have the Power to Do Friendship on Our Own Terms

Not only do many of us have more virtual Friends than real friends and are addicted to immediate gratification in connecting with others, we face another downside to social media: the power to define relationships on our own terms. Let me explain what this means. Let's say my friend Kevin texts me. I have some choices, don't I? I can read his text right away, or I can read it later. I can reply as soon as I read it, or I can reply later. I can even choose not to reply at all.

I have complete control over what I do—or what I don't do.

If my friend Sam posts a picture on Instagram, I have the power to determine several things. For example, is his picture Like-worthy? Is it worth the extraordinary inconvenience of double-tapping my finger on it? Or should I just scroll right on by? If this is another of Sam's stupid cat pictures, you can probably guess what I'm going to do.

I am in total and complete control of these friendships; I manage them from a distance. If you are my online friend, I'll show you only the parts of my life that I want you to see and tell you only what I want to tell you. If I don't want to respond to the things you choose to show me, I'm not going to. If you post too many pictures of your product, or too many duck-face selfies, or too many "inspirational quotes" that the person you credit may or may not have actually said (because you can't be bothered to check), or too many pictures of your cat making duck faces, I will unfollow you. We are in control of online friendships. And that control is changing how we manage our relationships.

Friendship doesn't mean what it used to mean.

2.4 NICE TO MEET YOU

At least a couple of times a year, I meet with some of the young leaders in our church to both invest in them and learn from them. The last time I met with this group, we talked for a long time about social media and relationships. One person said, "The more I use social media, the more I crave personal interaction."

I asked, "What about the rest of you? Is this true for all of you?" They unanimously agreed.

Another person said, "I feel more connected than ever before, yet I feel more alone."

So I asked them all, "Is this true for you?" Again, all of them nodded their heads in agreement.

It's almost like we're all lab rats, compulsively tapping a little button for food pellets: *scroll-scroll-scroll, click-click-click, scroll-scroll-scroll, click-click-click, scroll-scroll-scroll, click-click-click!* We sense that we want something more, but we just don't have the discipline to stop and really give ourselves the opportunity to engage in relationships we know we really want. Even worse, we don't know how to get from here to there.

I can't speak for you, but to be really honest, I have to admit that the more I dabble on social media, the more I realize I'm delaying the personal interaction I crave. I have also never been more connected and yet felt so alone.

The author of Hebrews wrote, "Let us think of ways to motivate one another to acts of love and good works" (Heb. 10:24 NLT). Wouldn't it be amazing to get together with other followers of Jesus and discuss this topic? We could start with, "Guys, how can we become so aggressive in how we show love to one other that other people really stop and think, 'Hey, those people must be Christians. Have you seen the way they love one another?'"

The writer of Hebrews goes on to say, "And let us not neglect commenting on one another's posts." Oh, wait, wait . . . I'm sorry. I totally messed that up.

No! He writes, "And let us not neglect our meeting together, as some people do, but encourage one another" (Heb. 10:25 NLT).

Really let that sink in: "Let us not neglect our meeting together."

"Let us not neglect our meeting together."

"Let us not neglect our *meeting together*."

Have we fallen out of this practice?

If this passage isn't enough to convince you, think about friendship in the context of your Christian faith. Think about what Jesus said: "For where two or three gather in my name, there am I with them" (Matt. 18:20). Isn't that powerful? Jesus promises us that whenever we come together with other believers in his name, we will experience his real presence in a supernatural way. Does that mean you can't experience his presence when you're alone? Absolutely not! You can. It's just that something more, something special, something powerful happens when we come together with other believers to seek God. When you join hands with someone, when you join your faith together and go before God on his throne, you experience his power and presence together in very real ways (Acts 16:25–26).

Something supernatural happens when we join together with other believers and lift up holy hands before our God to worship him (Ex. 17:10–13).

Something supernatural happens when we join together with other believers and, as believers have done for centuries, open up God's Word and read it aloud together (Neh. 8:1–12).

Something supernatural happens when we unite our faith and passionately seek God together in prayer (Acts 12:11–14).

Presence is powerful.

Think about it this way: God didn't shout his love from heaven. He showed his love on earth. He stripped himself of all heavenly glo-

> **God didn't shout his love from heaven. He showed his love on earth.**

ry and became one of us. God became flesh in the person of Jesus. Even one of Jesus' names, Immanuel, literally means "God with us." He came and lived with us. He loved people others rejected. He poured his heart into people who the religious community said were not worthy. He hung out with—and even ate with—tax collectors, sinners, and prostitutes.

2.5 PRESENT PERFECT

Presence is powerful. So why do so many of us settle for something less?

I'm going to suggest two practical things you can start doing right now that I promise will dramatically improve not just the quality of your relationships but our entire culture. Would you like to see God's Spirit present in your relationships? Then here's where you start.

Actually get together with people. Be physically present with one another. Not digitally. Not virtually. Not just in a group text, but in the same living room. Make the time to love people face to face, not just keyboard to keyboard. If you want to get really crazy, don't set a time limit on how long you'll hang out or what you'll discuss. In other words, just *be* with someone (not in the biblical sense, well, not unless you're married).

Paul told the Romans: "Don't just pretend to love others. Really love them" (Rom. 12:9 NLT). Don't just stay at that shallow level we've all become so used to. Paul continued: "Love each other with genuine affection, and take delight in honoring each other" (Rom. 12:10 NLT). He went on to say, "When

God's people are in need, be ready to help them" (Rom. 12:13 NLT). Love people. Really love them. Be present in their lives.

For example, imagine someone you know and love is hurting. Maybe they just received bad news, like a bad report from a doctor. Maybe they didn't get into the school they were hoping to attend. Or maybe they did, but now they're losing their scholarship. Maybe a boyfriend or girlfriend just broke up with them. Or a married friend just learned some terrible secret that their spouse had been keeping from them. Whatever difficulty a friend or loved one might be going through, what is an acceptable way you could show them love?

Many people might say just shooting out a text to them would be nice: "Hey, just thinking about you," or even, "Praying for you! Let me know if I can help."

But we can do better than that. If we're followers of Jesus and we want others to know us by how much we love one another, surely we can think of something else we could do. You know that device you use to text with? It might be hard to remember, but what's something else you can do with that device? That's right! You can actually *talk* on that thing. It's a lot harder, but maybe you could scroll through your contacts, find that person, tap their number, and call them on the phone. But what should you say? It's just so awkward. I recommend starting with this: "Hey, how are you doing?"

As they answer, you will actually be able to listen to what they're saying. You can hear the words *and* listen to the tone in their voice, which will also be communicating something. You might even ask if you can pray with your friend, right there over the phone. Then based on what they tell you, you can ask them a few more questions. I can promise you that a person-to-person conversation can go to amazing places that texting back and forth will not go.

A person-to-person conversation can go to amazing places that texting back and forth will not go.

Let's say you decide to get reeeally crazy—you want to take it to the next level. You don't just text. You don't just call. What's another way you can show love? You can actually go see them. Now, you might be thinking, "Whoa! Slow down there!" No, I'm serious. You could get in your car. You could fire up that scooter. Hop on your bike and start pedaling.

Just sit down with your friend, face to face. Ask a few questions, and then just listen. If it seems appropriate, maybe put your hand on their shoulder. Maybe even hold hands across the table and pray with them. And if they happen to start crying, well, that's probably okay and may be just what they need to do. You just wrap your arm around their shoulders. Or if you're a guy, punch them in the arm to cheer them up. Just let them know that you're right there in it with them.

Presence is powerful.

2.6 UNSPOKEN WORDS

When I was twenty-eight years old, we had just started our church, and another young family in the church experienced the tragic death of their three-year-old daughter. At the time, our daughter Catie was almost the same age as the daughter they lost. So it wasn't hard for me to imagine how horrible they must have felt.

I went to visit them at their home, and of course, I had no idea what to say. I was young and nervous and prayed in my car all the way over, "God, please give me the right words to say. This is so important, Father—please just help me not mess it up. Let me comfort them with your words, your love."

I will never forget what it was like to walk into that house. This dad, who was about my age, was crying about the little girl he had just lost. As I walked across the room toward where he was sitting, I tried to think about what I should say to him. But as I reached him, I couldn't even get a word out. So I did the next best thing: I sat down next to him and started crying. He had been crying softly, but it was as though my crying somehow gave him the permission, the freedom he needed to truly let loose. So we just sat there, crying together.

And it was a really "ugly cry." It was loud, and it was messy, and it was real. Two fathers with broken hearts.

After a few minutes, his wife came in and joined us. The three of us sat in their living room together, I have no idea for how long, sobbing and sobbing. I felt bad that was all I had to offer them. It was just that I could easily imagine losing my precious Catie—never getting to see her adorable smile again, never being able to look into those eyes as blue as the sky—and I could *feel* their pain inside of me, as if it were my own.

As our time together was winding down, I thought to myself, "I have to do something pastoral. Probably pray or something." So I prayed some pathetic little prayer. I don't remember any of the words I said, but it wasn't much of a prayer. They thanked me for coming, but I figured they were probably just being polite. I got in my car and drove away, completely ashamed of myself. I felt like the biggest spiritual failure. This family was in their greatest time of need, and I didn't say even one comforting thing.

Then a few days later, the most amazing thing happened. A note came in the mail from them. They wrote, "When you walked into the room, we just felt like God's love walked in with you." The note beautifully expressed how grateful they were that I came, how much it meant to them, and how much my visit had helped them. Then they wrote something I'll never forget: "Every word you said was just perfect."

Except for a short prayer, I didn't say a word! We just sat and cried together. How could that have been perfect? Then it dawned on me, a lesson I've never forgotten. Presence is powerful. My being with them, saying nothing during a time of indescribable sadness, communicated more than any words could have.

All of this happened before we had texting. But I want you to really think about this. Let's say I had sat down and collected my thoughts, really took the time to craft the perfect text, exactly the right words to say, tapped it all out, and hit send. Would that have been as meaningful to them? Not a chance. Even the perfect text could never mean anywhere nearly as much as presence.

2.7 GET ENGAGED

Being physically present is important. But if you're meeting with people just so you can check some box, so you can say, "Well, I tried. I went and met with other people, just like you said, but I guess maybe I'm just not really that type of person," then I can guarantee you, it's not going to make a difference in your life. Yes, be physically present. But be emotionally engaged too. Don't just be present; be all there.

"*Most important of all*, continue to show deep love for each other" (1 Peter 4:8 NLT, emphasis added).

Engage deeply. Go all in. Make sure that the person you're with is the most important person in the world when you're together.

My teenage daughters invite friends over, and they're all so excited as they're pouring into the house, chattering and laughing together. They head straight for some

> **Make sure that the person you're with is the most important person in the world when you're together.**

comfy room where they can all lounge around in big chairs or on the couch. They'll all sit down by each other—some of them even leaning against each other—and they'll each stare intently at their own tiny screens. They're alone together! But a teenage girl doesn't think anything of sending a text to her friend who's sitting right next to her.

We adults are no better. We've either seen, or if we're honest, we'll admit we've *been*, that family in the restaurant with each member glued to their phone or tablet—texting, gaming, emailing, surfing, whatever. We're losing the ability to relate to one another in natural ways.

If you're still not convinced about the severity of this problem, then imagine this. You and I are out having coffee somewhere. We've been engaged in conversation for a few minutes, and you're pouring your heart out to me. Then without warning, I reach down into my backpack and pull out a book. I open it to my bookmark and read a couple of pages. Then I put the bookmark back, close the book, put it away, and tell you, "Okay. Go on."

You'd think, "What's wrong with this guy?"

You start talking to me again, and I seem to be listening for a few minutes. But then I reach into my backpack again and pull out my to-do list and a pen. I jot a few notes down, mumbling to myself, "Gotta get butter. Call that repair guy back about the air conditioner. Wednesday: Get the car's oil changed."

I put the list back in my bag, look at you again, and say, "You were saying? Keep going. No, we're cool. Just keep going."

You start talking again, and after about five minutes—again without any warning—I simply stand up, walk over to someone else at another table, and say, "Hey, what's going on? It's good to see you. Oh, thanks! You too. You look great, man. Let's catch up sometime. Later."

Then I come back and sit down at our table again.

You'd think, "What is with this guy? Is he crazy? Is there something wrong with him? Could he be any ruder or more oblivious? Doesn't he have any social awareness? At least enough to make some small effort toward paying attention to me and attempting a conversation?"

Right? Do you see my point? This is exactly what we do with our phones—*all the time.* And we've become so used to interrupting normal, healthy communication with other activities and human beings that we somehow think this is okay. We're face-to-face with someone who matters to us, but instead of being with them the entire time, we're somewhere else virtually, digitally, electronically.

We're present, but we're not there.

2.8 MISSING PERSONS

Don't assume that I just don't understand or appreciate our world of tech. Hey, I have a smart phone too. And I'm just like you. Every time it buzzes, whistles, chirps, beeps, or dings, something in me can't help wondering,

"Oooh. What was that? I wonder if it's something important. Who sent me something? I must know right this instant."

Have you heard of FOMO? It's a thing. I read recently that FOMO was added to the latest edition of a popular English-language dictionary. FOMO is an acronym for Fear of Missing Out. It was coined for an entire generation of people who are constantly worried they're going to miss something.

We ask, "What am I missing?"

"I might miss someone's funny cat picture."

"I might miss the next video clip that goes viral. Then tomorrow everyone else will have seen it, and I'm gonna look like some kind of idiot because I haven't seen it yet."

"I might miss the next trailer for that movie that doesn't come out until eight months from now."

"I might miss a really beautiful inspirational quote from some person I've never heard of."

"I might miss someone Liking that picture I posted twenty minutes ago."

Ask yourself this question: at the end of your life, is it really going to matter how many Likes you got? Do you honestly believe that you're going to be lying on your deathbed one day thinking to yourself, "If I had gotten just three more Likes on that picture I posted of that weird tomato back in '15, I would have made an even hundred. One hundred Likes. Triple-digit Likes. Ooh, life would have been so good. #ICanDieHappy #RIPme."

> **Life is not about how many Likes you get. It is all about how much love you show.**

Life is not about how many Likes you get. It is all about how much love you show. The only way people will know that you are a follower of Jesus is by how well you love other people.

Have your children been begging for your attention? Have they been acting out? Maybe instead of posting online about how they're driving you crazy, you should put down the phone and engage them face-to-face. Maybe you argue, "Well, they're doing the same thing! I can't peel them away from that stupid device!" That may be true. But you're the parent. It's your job to teach your children how to engage in real life in ways that make it more meaningful than anything they can get looking at a screen and tapping pictures.

Instead of FOMO online, what you really should be afraid of is missing out on the people in front of you. You may be missing out on your children growing up. You may be missing out on enjoying an intimate marriage. You may be missing out on deep friendships filled with meaning. Is your fear that you're going to miss out on something causing you to miss out on what matters most?

Figuring this out in your own life is going to take a little effort on your part. (We'll go into specific details in chapter 8.) But maybe it's time for you to make some basic rules like these:

Phone curfew is 10:00 pm: phones get silenced and plugged in somewhere out of sight.

When you're with your family or close friends, phones get silenced so they don't even vibrate and are placed face down. Nobody picks up their phone during dinnertime or at your small group.

Really think this through. If you're in bed with your spouse while you're both on your phones, and you text her, "In the mood?" there's something wrong. She texts back, "Sry not tonite #headache." If you're not laughing at this, maybe it's because you can picture it happening—if it hasn't already.

"Dear children, let's not merely say that we love each other; let us show the truth by our actions" (1 John 3:18 NLT).

Don't just pray *for* people. Pray *with* them.

Don't just Like what they post. Like who they are.

Get involved in one another's lives.

The greatest weapon the first-century followers of Jesus had was their love for each other. The outside world persecuted them so fiercely that they were driven together into a radical, unifying love for one another. If anyone among them had a need, someone else sold some of their possessions and used the money to meet that need. Scripture says that they were so generous and so loving that "there were *no needy persons among them*" (Acts 4:32–37, emphasis added).

Can you imagine? The skeptical world looking on was thinking, "You know, I'm not so sure about that whole Jesus-being-raised-from-the-dead business. I'm not sure I believe what they believe, but I sure wish I had what they have. They love each other and care for each other."

That's exactly what Jesus said would happen: "Your love for one another will prove to the world that you are my disciples" (John 13:35 NLT).

They won't know that you're his disciple by how many followers you have.

They won't know that you're his disciple by how many Likes you get.

They won't know that you're his disciple by how quickly you respond to emails.

Believe it or not, they won't even know that you're his disciple by how many Bible verses you post.

No, they will know that you're Jesus' disciple when they see his love in you through your actions. When you get involved in the lives of other people, when you care for them right where they are, when you open up your heart and do life with them—that's when they'll see something in you that they really want. Then when they ask you what makes you so different from everybody else, you'll be able to say, "God gave his Son for me to forgive me of my sins. I've found freedom and life in him, and that's how I'm able to show you this kind of love."

Others won't know you by your Likes.

They will know you by his love.

Chapter 3

REVEALING AUTHENTICITY

The Struggle with Control

Honesty and transparency make you vulnerable. Be honest and transparent anyway.

Mother Teresa

I have two buddies that I would call best friends. If I needed something, both of them would be there for me any time of the day or night. But even these guys don't know everything about me. Yeah, we're tight, but some things I just don't share with anyone. I wish I could, especially with some of my struggles, some of my fears. But you know, it just seems too risky. I'm afraid if I told them everything about me, it would be too much, too embarrassing, or just too awkward. So we just keep hanging out. But inwardly it still bothers me because I know I'm holding back.

Gary T.

I don't know how many times I've thought I really "knew" someone. I'd meet someone, and in no time we were like the best of
friends. I used to open up about everything. You know, the boys
I like. What I dream about. What scares me. But each time I do, it
seems like I get hurt. I always thought we'd be friends, but something always happens to ruin everything. Then they know my
secrets, and it makes me feel too vulnerable. So I'm more guarded
nowadays. It's lonelier, but it also makes me feel safer.

Morgan A.

Everyone thinks I'm so perfect, which I guess is what I want them
to think. People love what I post on Pinterest. And on social media,
well, I know how to make things look good. I take pictures in
my house only after it's been cleaned and picked up. I snap only
"candids" of my kids when their clothes match and their hair is
combed. My husband and I go out only every couple of months,
but I'll take several different shots and post them over time to
make it look like we go out more than we do. I never lie about it.
But I never let everyone know it's from the same night out. My life
is so not what it looks like. I feel overwhelmed all the time. And I
wish my husband and I were a lot closer.

Julie J.

3.1 SMILE FOR THE CAMERA

If you're like me, then I expect you remember the same worst day of the entire school year as I do: picture day. Picture day was horrible! It was the only day of the year I'd ever bring a comb to school or remotely think about what I wore. When they'd call me out of class to go sit for my picture, I'd stop by the bathroom on the way to do a little last-minute prep in the mirror: fluff my hair in the back, straighten up the part down the center, get the wings up on both sides, practice my most "natural" smile a few times—you know the drill.

With a final sigh, I'd head for the room where the photographer had set up shop, usually in the school library. You could count on at least one giant black umbrella with a huge light radiating heat at least a thousand degrees and some really fake landscape.

But the worst was that you'd get just one shot—one take, and one take only. The photographer's "One, two, *three!*" was immediately followed by a blinding flash. It didn't matter if you were looking the wrong way or had something in your teeth, or that your shirt had some unfortunate wrinkle that made you look like you had a third nipple. That was your legacy. That one picture would define your entire sixth-grade year for all eternity.

Actually, that wasn't the worst part. No, the very worst thing was that you had no idea what your picture looked like. You had no instant gratification from some little digital screen you could check. They'd just send you back to your classroom, and you'd have to wait *weeks*—sometimes even a couple of *months*—for the pictures to come. And if your parents didn't have enough money to buy one of the photographer's stupid plan packages when your pictures came, you wouldn't know what yours looked like until you saw it in the yearbook! Can you feel my pain? I'm telling you, most people today can't even imagine!

But things are different now.

You don't have to go on picture day to get your school photo taken. And you definitely don't have to wait long—maybe a few seconds—to see how the photo turned out. With so many ways to post pictures on social media, you don't even have to be a school kid to get excited about sharing as many as you want with all your virtual friends. You don't even need a good reason to take a picture and post it; just *wanting* to do it is reason enough.

Which brings us to one of the most interesting aspects of technology and social media: the selfie.

3.2 ALL BY MY SELFIE

When I was a kid, we didn't have selfies. Even the word is relatively new. It simply refers to any picture you take of your*self*, usually with a mobile or smart phone. Most people post selfies online to show off something to their friends: the fun thing they're doing, the cool people they're hanging out with, the new clothes they're wearing, or even just how good they happen to look and feel.

While selfies have been around for a few years, coinciding mostly with the introduction of smart phones and social networks, the selfie phenomenon seems to keep building momentum. As of October, 2013, on various forms of social media, people had posted forty-one million pictures that included the hashtag #Selfie somewhere in the caption. You read that right: forty-one *million*.[5] And that number continues to explode. The selfie hashtag has since grown more than 200 percent in usage since January of 2013 (at which time it wasn't even in the top 100 most commonly used hashtags on Instagram).[6]

> It's no exaggeration to say we've become a selfie-obsessed culture.

It's no exaggeration to say we've become a selfie-obsessed culture.

You can take a picture of yourself, and if you need to touch it up a little, you can apply a filter. Most smart phones now have filter tools that let you fix those little problem areas. You can change the color saturation, brighten the image, soften it, or make it black and white. You can even get rid of red-eye and erase that second chin! You can even change the color of your eyes and raise your cheekbones.

When I was a kid, if you happened to have a zit on picture day, you had to live with it captured in glossy color for the rest of your life. Now you can just edit that unsightly reality right out and change history! We can even filter our lives and tell people, "This is the photoshopped me that I want you to see."

3.3 STRENGTH IN NUMBERS

I have a workout partner who doesn't use social media. He's always rolling his eyes and shaking his head at people who spend so much of their time playing with their phones. Recently when I arrived for a workout, he came rushing out of the locker room and said, "Craig, come quick! You gotta see this! There's a guy with his phone doing that, that thing you were telling me about!"

Although I wasn't sure what he was talking about, I followed him into the locker room and looked in the direction he was pointing toward the mirrors. Sure enough, there stood a young guy, probably in his early twenties, without a shirt on, posing and flexing and snapping picture after picture of himself in the mirror. He held his phone way up high to get the best angle (I guess), took a deep breath, then flexed his entire body as he exhaled, clicking dozens of shots. But what made the whole scene so bizarre, so amazing, so entertaining, was that he just kept doing it. Over and over and over. And over.

At first, my friend and I were the only ones watching. But then a couple of other guys came up beside us to enjoy the spectacle. Soon a small crowd of curious spectators had gathered (even Old Naked Locker Room Guy came over), almost a dozen guys of various ages, all of us strangely fascinated by this one young guy's concentration, his relentless determination, to capture his muscle-bound chest in hundreds of selfies.

After what seemed like several minutes, I went to my locker, changed into my workout clothes, and ran into a guy from church. We stood there and visited for probably three or four minutes, then said goodbye. By this time, at least seven or eight minutes had passed. But as I walked around the corner to head out to the weight room, guess who was still there?

#SelfieMuscleMan was still going at it!

But what this guy was doing isn't really all that unusual. He is just a reflection of the selfie-centered world we live in now. We take picture after picture of ourselves until we can get the perfect one, and then we apply a filter, maybe use an app to edit or crop as needed until we get the image just like we want it.

Selfies seem harmless enough, but I'm starting to wonder how our selfie-obsession might be changing how we relate to one another. For example, the more filtered our lives become—the more we show others only the "me" we want them to see—the more difficulty we have being authentic. One recent study links an alarming increase in plastic surgery to patients' desires to get the "perfect selfie."[7]

The more filtered our lives become—the more we show others only the "me" we want them to see—the more difficulty we have being authentic.

But you know what the strangest thing is? Our culture keeps telling us that all of this is perfectly acceptable. After you've filtered your picture, you have to take the time to create the perfect caption. It has to be clever, but not *too* clever. While you have to get it just right, you have to make it *look* like you're not trying too hard. Then you have to choose exactly the right hashtag to achieve maximum impact. After all, you're about to put your filtered self out there so the rest of the world can affirm you.

But before long, you might find yourself wondering whether they would like the real you.

3.4 OFF SCRIPT

Pictures aren't the only things we're becoming used to controlling, thanks to technology and social media. We have the luxury of sending an article, text, tweet, or email to virtually anyone we want to communicate with. And we can edit and revise as much as we want before we hit send.

The problem, however, is that many of us have filtered our messages so much that we are no longer comfortable with real, unscripted, spontaneous conversation. We've become so used to the luxury of being able to edit the things we say that some of us really struggle when we have to have normal, everyday conversations with and in front of real, live human beings. Technology has given us tools that are unprecedented in human history, but an entire generation is growing up uncomfortable in conversations they cannot control.

I recently met with a group of young adults to talk about how they structure their social lives, including how they use technology daily in their relationships. All of them said that when their cell phone rings, they're more likely *not* to answer than to answer. Every one would look to see who is calling and then decide whether they want to talk to that person.

It's interesting to me that when I was their age, the option to answer based on the caller didn't even exist! I can remember when "caller ID" became an expensive option you could add to your landline home phone. Before that technological marvel, you didn't have any idea who was calling when your phone rang. You had to answer the call to find out who was on the other end. Then you had to actually talk to them! Can you imagine?

You had no idea what this person was going to say, or even what they might ask. So you learned to think on your feet and about social expectations and everyday etiquette. I remember my parents teaching me "proper phone etiquette" as part of learning overall "good manners." (Rule number one: never say Mom or Dad can't talk right now because they're using the bathroom.)

But today we have the luxury—hard to say whether it's a blessing or a curse—of being able to decide whether we want to answer a call based on factors that we control. We can see a call come in, send it directly to voice mail, wait for the person to finish leaving a message, and then immediately listen to the voice mail or wait until later.

We have even more choices about responding. We can call the person back or not call back. But what do many of us do? Respond with a text message. Why? Because a text lets us stay in control. We don't have to talk—to experience all of that unnecessary anxiety of not knowing where a conversation might go. We don't have to have a "conversation" at all if we don't want to.

When I was talking with the young adults, I asked, "Do you feel uncomfortable having conversations?"

One young woman answered, "Sure. Sometimes. Especially if they're unplanned. I get really nervous about having to talk on the phone. So sometimes I'll script out what I'm going to say before I call somebody."

I could hardly believe it. I said, "Really? Like what kinds of phone conversations would you script? When would you do that?"

She said, "Well, let's say I'm going to call to order a pizza or something. I'll write out the whole thing: I'm going to say 'hello' first, and here's what they'll probably say, so here's what I'll say next, all the way through. It just really makes me nervous to talk on the phone."

As it turned out, her approach was not particularly unusual. I asked the other twenty-five young adults there, "What about you guys? How many of you would script a phone call for something like ordering a pizza?" Probably 75 percent of them raised their hands.

This shouldn't surprise me. This generation simply hasn't been required to learn to communicate in unfiltered ways. They've gotten so used to being in complete control of their end of a conversation that even the idea of giving up some of that control is unsettling. They have their filter on all the time.

But here's the catch. While these young adults may experience the effects of today's technology more acutely, we are all affected by it. We are all forgetting how to have everyday conversations. We are all filtering and editing our lives, and the more we do, the more difficulty we have being authentic.

And if we can't be real, are we really living?

3.5 BEHIND THE VEIL

Strangely, it isn't technology alone that causes this kind of control/avoidance response. This isn't even a modern problem; it has been going on as long as people have existed:

> We are not like Moses, who would put a veil over his face to prevent the Israelites from seeing the end of what was passing away. But their minds were made dull, for to this day the same veil remains when the old covenant is read. It has not been removed, because only in Christ is it taken away. Even to this day when Moses is read, a veil covers their hearts. But whenever anyone turns to the Lord, the veil is taken away. Now the Lord is the Spirit, and where the Spirit of the Lord is, there is freedom. And we all, who with unveiled faces contemplate the Lord's glory, are being transformed into his image with ever-increasing glory, which comes from the Lord, who is the Spirit.
>
> —*2 Corinthians 3:13–18*

In this passage, Paul is trying to show the Corinthians how much greater the new covenant is (freedom through Christ) than the old covenant (adherence to the law). He is referring to a story in the Old Testament found in Exodus 34:29–35. Moses had gone to the top of Mount Sinai where God gave him the Ten Commandments. He spent forty days on the mountain with God, and when he came down, Moses' face was glowing—because he had been in the presence of the glory of God! (The closest I've gotten to this is that sometimes when I'm preaching really hard, my face might start glowing with sweat.)

I used to think when I read this story that Moses put on the veil to protect the people from the fear-inspiring glory of God on his face. But if we look more closely at the text, we see that he used the veil not to protect the people but to keep them from seeing that *the glory was fading.* Even Moses, after seeing the glory of God, didn't want others to know he was losing the image.

Paul then makes a comparison (2 Cor. 3:14–16). When the old covenant was read, the Jewish people who didn't believe could not see the truth. Why? Because their unbelief blinded them like a veil. But anyone who turns to Christ understands the truth, because he removes this veil and reveals God's glory.

You might wonder how this passage applies to us today. Well, most of us put on a veil of some kind or another to hide the truth about ourselves. We've become skilled at filtering our lives, showing others only what we want them to see. This is similar to what Paul implies Moses did; he hid from the people the fact that God's glory was fading away.

> We've become skilled at filtering our lives, showing others only what we want them to see.

This tendency is part of our sinful nature. When we're insecure, when we don't feel good about ourselves, and perhaps most of all when we sin, instead of confessing, which would set us free and heal us, we tend to hide, to put on a veil, to filter our lives.

This behavior goes all the way back to the garden of Eden when Adam and Eve sinned against God. They didn't immediately say, "God, we're so sorry. We shouldn't have done that." No, Genesis 3:7–10 says they were ashamed because they realized they were naked. They were afraid, so they covered themselves with fig leaves and hid, perhaps thinking something like, "We don't want God to see the real us." All of us behave in similar ways, whether on social media or in other relationships. We create various versions of ourselves in order to impress, manipulate, or control others as much as possible.

So how can we find the courage to remove our veils, reveal the truth about ourselves, and experience the freedom to be ourselves? Paul tells us, "Whenever anyone turns to the Lord, the veil is taken away" (2 Cor. 3:16–18). We can't do this by ourselves. Only Christ can take away the veil.

3.6 TOE BE OR NOT TOE BE

I feel very thankful that I've found freedom from something I hid behind a veil for too long. I was in bondage to the approval of people. But by the power and grace of God, I now have total and complete freedom . . . about my toes. It's true! I have caveman feet. I wear size twelve shoes, and about 40 percent of my feet is toes. My toes are so big, each one has a unique personality.

For as long as I can remember, my toes have been my worst physical feature. I was so embarrassed about them that I went to a lot of trouble to keep them hidden. My wife, Amy, and I are in complete agreement about this policy. I could never ask for a better wife, but even she says, "Craig, I love everything about you. You are perfect in every way. I love you from the top of your head to the bottom of your ankles."

She knows my feet are the ugliest ever. Sometimes she'll remind me, "Be sure you put socks on before you come into our bedroom."

This scenario has played out many times at our house: I'll be sitting on the couch, watching something on TV or reading a book, in just a pair of shorts—no shirt, no socks, no shoes. If the doorbell rings, my wife never says, "Put on a shirt!"

She says, "Cover up your feet! Whoever that is, I don't want them to see your toes!"

She's not being mean. She's just being honest.

For years, I've been self-conscious about my toes. You'd probably be surprised how jealous I can be of people who can wear flip-flops. I never even wore sandals, and I envied people whose toes could bask uncovered in the sunlight.

Finally this past year I had a breakthrough. For the first time ever, I thought, "I'm in my midforties. I'm happily married. My wife loves almost every part of me. Why should I care what anybody else thinks?"

So I bought myself a pair of sandals. And I wear them without shame. I've worn them to restaurants. I've worn them to the park. Sure, occasionally little kids will scream and cry and run away, but where the Spirit of the Lord is, there is freedom! And I have been set free.

I'm exaggerating—but only a little. This may seem like a silly thing to you, but it has honestly been a struggle in my life for decades. It is the absolute truth that I veiled my toes because I was afraid of what people might think if they saw them and how ridiculous they look. So let me ask you, in all seriousness:

What veils are you wearing? I mean it. What image are you trying to project in your life that doesn't reflect the real you?

Social media practically trains us to present a self that isn't honest.

> **Social media practically trains us to present a self that isn't honest.**

It entices us to say, "I'm Spiritual Guy! Here's a screen capture from my phone of the YouVersion Bible App's Verse of the Day!"

Or, "I'm Spiritual Girl! Here's a picture of my cup of coffee, with my Bible open right next to it! See my highlighter? See my journal? I'm so holy—and humble!"

But in the reality of your everyday life, you may be keeping the secret of an ongoing sin. No one knows about it. You've never confessed it to a single soul. Part of you hopes you'll just be able to hide it forever. But it's there, every day, haunting you, messing with your head, making you crazy.

Maybe you project an image on Pinterest that says, "I'm Super Mom! Look at this picture of the huge pile of amazing things I baked for my third grader's fundraiser at school! Here I am with all three of my kids at soccer practice! Look how cute their clothes are! And how clean their faces are! And they all have snacks! And they're all smiling!"

Meanwhile in your everyday real life, you feel overwhelmed. You feel like you're probably a bad mother because even though you do all these things for your kids, you're exhausted a lot of the time. You feel overworked. And you certainly don't have time for any relationships in addition to your family—like friends. You feel like you don't have a life. Based on the outside, everyone thinks you're amazing. But they can't see the inside, where you feel like you're beginning to crumble.

Or maybe your Facebook page says, "Check me out! I'm the Good Dad! Here's a selfie of me and my kid at the skate park! And here I am at my little girl's recital! Here I am, pushing two kids at a time on swings! This is what a Good Dad is supposed to look like! (Right?)"

But the real you feels like a failure as a dad. You know you're working too much, but it's the only way to give them the life you want them to have. You're busy all the time and distracted, always thinking about other things, so that even when you're with your family, you're not really with them. Sometimes your temper gets the best of you, and you're short with them.

Maybe your Instagram photos say, "We're Anniversary Couple! Just look at how happy we are together! See that sunset behind us? We're bestest friends! I wuv my widdle smoochie-pookins! We have the best marriage ever!"

But just five minutes earlier, you were arguing about where to stand for the picture. You didn't even want to take that picture. You hate that shirt. You wore it only because she made you because she gave it to you for your birthday.

And she's thinking you are just so ungrateful. Nothing she does for you ever feels like it's good enough. She never asks you for anything. Why do you always seem so angry?

Our modern ability to manage our image encourages and makes it easier for us to wear veils that cover up the truth.

3.7 THE QUIET GAME

People have told me that the only reason they posted a picture was because they had to post *something*.

Have you ever thought, "Let's see . . . It's not #tbt (throwback Thursday), so I can't just use an old picture. I'm gonna have to come up with something new. Hmm . . . What could I do that would make a good picture? I guess we could go out to dinner. We can't really afford that right now, but at least we'd have something we could photograph and post!"

#HowCrazyIsThat? Many of us are making life choices just to create a string of social media moments, and all because we want to show some imaginary life that we think people want to see.

That sort of raises the question, "So, Craig, are you saying that we should always be only 100 percent honest and show everything we do on social media?" Yes and no. Yes, we should always try to be honest. But no, we should not show everything on social media. I like Beth Moore's perspective: "Be authentic with all. Transparent with most. And intimate with some."

For example, if I tweet on Saturday afternoon just before I preach the Saturday evening service, "I'm so excited about this message! I can hardly wait!" That's actually true.

But believe me, plenty of times I do *not* tweet what is true. That doesn't mean that I lie in a tweet. That means I simply choose not to share what I'm thinking. For example, I was recently thinking, "I'm exhausted. I'm in a bad mood. I haven't had a day off since I can't remember when. I don't even know if this message I'm about to preach makes sense! And besides, the state fair is going on. Half of the church is going to be riding the Zipper, looking at cows, and eating fried butter!"

Here's the bottom line: Everything you say must be true, but not everything true should be said. If I post something, it must be the truth, but we don't need to share everything on social media. Some people are oversharers. You know some, right? They say too much, and you want to tell them to "shutteth thine trap." Not everybody wants to know all of your feelings about every person you know.

A woman once wrote on my Facebook page, "Pray for my husband, _____." Let's just think this through. Right there on my

> **Everything we say must be true, but not everything true should be said.**

page, which is public, is her name with her little picture right next to it. And right there in her post, she included his whole name. She also explained, "He is the biggest jerk who's ever lived. I can't stand him. I don't want to be married to him another day. Unless the Lord Jesus Christ redeems his soul, I have no place in my heart for this man. Please pray for my husband."

By the way, I did pray for her husband. I prayed for him because he's married to her! What she did was not smart. It was not helpful. And it was not productive. Be wise about what you post.

So yes, we should remove our veils and tell the truth. But social media is not the place to bare all! Be yourself, but don't feel like you have to share everything you're feeling. Being authentic is not about being brutally honest and confrontational about everything on your mind. But by all means—at the right time, with the right people, and when you're face to face—drop the veil completely. If you don't, you'll always be longing for something more.

When you put on the veil and post something hoping for Likes, hoping for affirmation, even if you receive it, you're still going to feel empty because you're not being real with people *about yourself.* But the place to be vulnerable is where God wants you to be vulnerable: in the context of private, life-giving, healthy, God-honoring relationships.

"But their minds were made dull . . . a veil covers their hearts" (2 Cor. 3:14–15). Notice this: a veil that first covers the face eventually covers the heart. It begins as just a superficial covering, a temporary attempt to cover up a problem rather than addressing it head-on. But left unchecked, the hidden problem will become a serious spiritual condition.

3.8 SURRENDER YOUR SELFIES

It's time to remove the veils and take off the filters. But doing so won't be easy. You may have some secrets that you've kept hidden for decades. You may have veils on veils on veils. You may be acting the part and playing the role, but in your heart of hearts, you know you're not the person you present to the world.

The danger is that we can become so used to showing our filtered self, so accustomed to the half-truths and exaggerations, that we don't even know who our real self is anymore. Are you one person in one group of people and a different person in another group? Until you show who you really are, until you know and are fully known, you're going to be longing for something more.

When we're always filtered, when every selfie shows only our best side, we may impress some people some of the time. They may think, "Based on this tweet, I really like this guy." But that's not real. You're not really connecting with them. They're not connecting with you. We want so badly to connect with others, and we think the best way to do so is by showing off our strengths. But it doesn't work that way. Here's why:

We actually connect with people through our weaknesses. We may impress them with our strengths, but we connect through our weaknesses.

Let me explain what I mean. Have you ever met someone, mentally looked them over, and considered the life you think they have? They're nice looking for their age. Their spouse is attractive. They seem to have great kids. Their life seems to be together. In so many ways, it looks to you like they're living your dreams. What do you think? "They're just . . . so . . . perfect. I don't think I like them!" Right?

Isn't that tempting to do? But after you've spent more time with them and seen them in many different circumstances, you begin to get to know them, and you realize, "Oh. I never would have thought they struggle with some of the same things I do. They're human after all. You know what? I really like these guys!"

Why? Because we connect through weaknesses.

Now that we're on the same page about these #struggles, what do we do? Where do we go from here? How do we "turn off" our desire to constantly filter who we show the world we are? Usually this is the part of a chapter where I try to give you some practical advice. I could give you really sound, straightforward suggestions like:

- Don't use a filter every time on your photos.
- Try not to care so much about what people think.
- If your toes are long, don't be ashamed. Put on a pair of sandals, and let's hang out.

All of this qualifies as solid advice. But the truth is you can get advice like this anywhere. I'd much rather give you godly advice, wisdom that can come only from the source: God's Word. I can give the solution to the problems in this entire chapter with one simple phrase. If you don't take anything else away, I want to make sure you get this: only Christ can remove the veil.

That's it. When we turn to Christ, he removes the veil.

Maybe you're exhausted. You're weary because you've already tried everything else you can think of. You've looked everywhere you can for affirmation. You've turned to one person after another, but you still haven't found that thing you're longing for. This is the promise you have from God, straight from his Word: You don't have to remove the veil. When you turn to Christ, he does it for you!

Then you can finally drop the mask because you're not getting your approval from Likes; you're getting it from his love. You will no longer be living *for* the approval of people; you will be living *from* the approval of God. He will reveal the truth: you are acceptable to God through Jesus. You are the righteousness of God in Christ. His grace, his righteousness, is sufficient for you.

When you realize that Christ is all you have, you'll also find that he's all you need. You don't need approval from someone else because you have approval from Christ. When you turn to Jesus, you have the same Spirit that raised him from the dead living within you. Your identity is not connected to how many followers you can get. Your identity comes from who you are following, and you are following Jesus.

> Your identity comes from who you are following, and you are following Jesus.

"Now the Lord is the Spirit, and where the Spirit of the Lord is, there is freedom. And we all, who with unveiled faces contemplate the Lord's glory, are being transformed into his image with ever-increasing glory, which comes from the Lord, who is the Spirit" (2 Cor. 3:17–18).

Have you ever experienced the Spirit of God? Have you ever called out to him? Asked him to come and live inside of you? When you do, you experience freedom. When we all let the veils fall—because our lives are better when we're together, when we act as the body of Christ, when we allow each other to see the "real" us—we will truly see the Lord's glory.

Why? Because it's not about you and me. It's not about our selfies. The reason we exist is to give *him* glory. When we do, this Scripture says we will begin to be transformed—not into the person we think others want us to be but into *his image,* bringing *ever-increasing glory.*

Turn to Christ.

He'll take your veil away.

He'll transform you into the image of Christ, not for the approval of people but for the glory of God. We're not called to elevate ourselves (John 3:30); we're called to deny ourselves and follow him (Luke 9:23–24). The way to follow Jesus in a selfie-centered world is to give him glory in all that we do.

Surrender your selfies.

Let Jesus lift your veil.

Chapter 4

RESURRECTING COMPASSION

The Struggle with Desensitization

Compassion is the knowledge that there can never really be any peace and joy for me until there is peace and joy finally for you too.

Frederick Buechner

After my granddad died, I went online and posted about how sad I felt. Within minutes all my friends commented and told me they loved me, that they'd be praying for me, and stuff like that. It made me feel really good at the time. But then later when I saw my friends, no one mentioned it. Not one person asked me about my grandfather's death or about how I was doing. Not one. It made me feel like my friends don't really care.

Meagan M.

I get so sick of everyone posting about the latest big thing. Just last week, a guy from work was raising money for his neighbor's daughter who has leukemia. Another person needed money for a mission trip to Tegucigalpa, Honduras (for the second time this year). And this one lady from our small group posts stories every week about human trafficking. I know all these things are important, but they're just not my thing. I feel bad sometimes, but I really wish people wouldn't talk about this kind of stuff all the time.

Rob V.

We'd been friends since high school, so I thought we'd be friends forever. I can't believe she doesn't want to talk to me anymore. I knew it was a big deal when she posted that her mom had lung cancer. It wasn't a huge surprise to me because I remember her mom smoking, like, two packs a day whenever I stayed over. Knowing it was a big deal, I commented on her Facebook post to tell her I was praying. Then I even sent her a text later that day to tell her I was sorry. But now she's furious because that's all I did. Evidently she expected me to call or visit her. I would have done more, but I just got so busy. She thinks I just don't care. I think she's being a bit of a baby.

Marla K.

4.1 TAKE THE [LATEST CAUSE] CHALLENGE

In 2012, a marketing company adopted a current cause—vulnerable children in a war-torn country being kidnapped and turned into soldiers—and designed a campaign to raise awareness. When they launched their mission, people all over the world passionately took up the rallying cry, "Kony 2012!" For days, weeks even, it seemed like this campaign was all anybody talked about. It was everywhere online and picked up in the news cycles. After a few months, the producer who was the mastermind behind the whole thing fell into some personal challenges, and that was in the news for a week or so. Then the whole thing—Kony 2012 and the news about its producer—just went away.

More recently, two hundred schoolgirls were kidnapped by a militant group in Nigeria and disappeared into the jungle. A handful managed to escape over the first week or so and told their harrowing story, which captured the heart of the world. Everyone was talking about it:

- "Oh my goodness! It's so terrible!"
- "Somebody should do something!"
- "Governments need to act!"
- "They need to send in special forces!"
- "Everybody needs to sign this petition."
- "Share this everywhere!"

As I'm writing this, tragically, all of those girls are still missing. But I don't know anyone who is still talking about them, still sharing, still urging others to do something. It was hot. Until it wasn't anymore.

You may also remember the ALS Ice Bucket Challenge. For several weeks, the internet was clogged with video after video of everyone you knew getting ice water dumped on their heads. All of your friends and family, celebrities, talk show hosts, people in costumes, people in exotic locations, children, and even pets. ALS, amyotrophic lateral sclerosis, probably better known by its popular name, Lou Gehrig's disease, was something people knew about but weren't necessarily discussing. Within weeks, the ALS Ice Bucket Challenge raised millions of dollars for ALS research. And then it vanished almost as quickly as it had exploded onto the scene.

There's no question that social media offers us all kinds of benefits when it comes to helping others. But I would like you to consider that it also presents many downsides. In particular, evidence seems to indicate a strong correlation between sharing popular ideas and the decline of compassion as a shared cultural value. Some cause or crisis shifts into the spotlight of popular culture for a brief fifteen minutes of fame. Then people lose interest in it when something else comes along, as if this new thing somehow means the first issue is no longer significant or worth pursuing. It's as if anything that becomes popular is easily discarded. It might be interesting for a while, but then no one wants to touch it again when they move on to the next big and popular thing.

> **Evidence seems to indicate a strong correlation between sharing popular ideas and the decline of compassion as a shared cultural value.**

The University of Michigan conducted a comprehensive study of attitudes among college students between 1979 and 2009. Over that thirty-year period, the researchers observed a drastic decline in empathy. Basically, they found that students today care about others 40 percent less than people did during the 1980s.[8]

Do you know what I find most tragic? You might not even care.

Does the meaning of this change in empathy strike a chord of concern deep within you? Does it even register?

4.2 SELFIE-CENTERED

I was curious about how the researchers arrived at the conclusion of a 40 percent drop in how much young people care about other people. So I did a little research into their research. They interviewed each participant using a set of statements, asking the students to indicate on a numbered scale how strongly they felt about each statement. Here are two examples of the kinds of statements they used to measure empathy:

1. "I sometimes try to understand my friends better by imagining how things look from their perspective."

2. "I often have tender, concerned feelings for people less fortunate than myself."

Responses to these statements on average were 40 percent lower in the 2009 group than they were in the 1979 group. A decline was apparent for the first few years of the study, but responses really dropped around the time social media began to be a cultural phenomenon. These researchers argue that a rise in the use of technology very likely directly causes a decline in empathy.

Why would engaging more with social media cause young people to care less about other people? As you might expect, there are many theories. Let's examine four possible reasons.

First, consider how most forms of social media make us more obsessed with ourselves. Call it narcissism, vanity, or just plain old being full of ourselves. However we dress it up, social media can quickly promote us to the level of someone important, someone who has something to say, to share, to show, to shout. And we can find no more glaring example than the obsession over selfies.

We discussed selfies in chapter 3, and if you're younger, the word *selfie* isn't new to you. It's been a part of your vocabulary for so long that it's a normal part of everyday life. Remember, a *selfie* is a picture you take *of yourself.* But for decades, this practice was not the norm.

Like me, maybe you assume that taking selfies is a simple, straightforward activity: you just snap a nice picture of yourself smiling. But it's not that simple. There are all kinds of popular styles of selfies, and the list keeps growing. Here are a few of my favorites (to catalog, not to take!):

- *The Driving in My Car Selfie.* Level of difficulty: low to medium. Bonus points are awarded for clever, funny, or unusual things in the background.

- *The Duck-Face Selfie.* Level of difficulty: extremely high. I can't really say why, but this one seems to be much more popular among girls and young women than it is among boys and men. Probably because when guys do it, it looks like they're just trying too hard.

- *The Me and My #bff Selfie.* (jsyk—just so you know—#bff stands for "best friends forever," also commonly known as a "bestie.") Level of difficulty: medium. Generally requires several takes to capture both faces in sync with each other.

- *The Kissing Somewhere Cool Selfie.* #oohlala (self-explanatory). Level of difficulty: picture, medium, but difficulty of reaching location, high to extremely high. The harder it is to reach the location, or the more exotic it is, the more #epic the picture.

- *The Me with My Pet Selfie.* This one is pretty self-explanatory. The younger the animal in the picture, the higher the bonus points.

- *The We've Got Great Seats at the Big Game While You're Home Alone Selfie.* This one is also pretty self-explanatory. While the bonus point system for this one is complicated, it has mostly to do with capturing recognizable players in the background.

- *The Me with My Food Selfie.* An Instagram staple, the main idea here is to incite strong responses—jealousy, disgust, salivation, etc.—among your followers. This is one of the rare cases where followers may actually Like the post and also include a comment that says something like, "Hating you rn." While *rn* may *look* like it should mean registered nurse, it is actually the abbreviated form of the phrase "right now."

- *The Rocking This Outfit Selfie.* This is another field dominated by young girls and women, although men seem to be making a valiant effort to catch up. Bonus points if you can get your shoes in the picture too. #youwish.

I know this is all kind of overwhelming, especially if you've never even heard of this phenomenon before, but what's really scary is that these categories are only the tip of the iceberg. I didn't even get into the Just Woke Up Selfie, the New 'Do Selfie (for a new haircut), the Restaurant Birthday Sombrero Selfie, and countless others. But you see the common denominator here, don't you?

It's all about you.

Social media encourages us—I'd say it even *trains* us—to become more narcissistic, more full of ourselves. One study I read indicated that 80 percent of what a user posts on social media is directly related to that user's own immediate interests.[9] On the one hand, this makes sense. Think about it. If I'm interested in something, I'm more likely to think you'll be. And then consider what we look at habitually. It's often what people are saying about us. We ask, "Are people Liking my posts? Are people commenting on the things I've posted? What can I do to attract more of the kind of positive affirmation I enjoy?"

> Social media actually trains our bodies—like little laboratory rats tapping a feeder bar—to become more and more and more self-centered over time.

Why do we do this? It's emotional, sure, but it also involves science and chemicals. As I mentioned earlier, every time we see something about ourselves—especially things we perceive as positive—our brains release dopamine. That rush gives us a little (completely legal) buzz, a little "A-ha! I like this!" moment. When we look at social media, when we participate in it, both posting and casually surfing, it's actually training us—training our bodies like little laboratory rats tapping a feeder bar—to become more and more and more self-centered over time. But how does social media cause us to care less about other people? By transforming our bodies to be more self-centered.

We are more obsessed with ourselves than ever.

4.3 ALL THINGS ARE NOT EQUAL

Why would social media cause us to care less about other people? First, it turns pain into popular causes that are easily abandoned. Second, it makes us more obsessed with ourselves. Third is an equally serious problem: constantly using social media conditions us to care less about other people because we become desensitized over time. Without our even realizing it, social media can become a drain on our wellspring of human compassion. When we see pain all the time, all those sad things in our feed over and over again, our natural coping mechanisms numb us to the pain. The more often we see pain, the harder it is for us to care each time we're exposed to it.

> The more often we see pain in our social media feeds, the harder it is for us to care each time we're exposed to it.

Let me give you an example. Years ago, if I was channel surfing and came across some commercial or program showing a sweet-looking, malnourished child with flies buzzing around her face, my heart stopped. These images usually bothered me so much that I'd immediately change the channel. I couldn't stand the feeling of guilt seeing another human being in pain as I sat in my comfortable, air-conditioned home watching on a big, flat screen TV.

But after a while, I had seen so many of these images that they simply didn't bother me as much. They became like any commercial we see over and over again; after the first few viewings, they become invisible. Repeating a stimulus causes it to register less and less each time we're exposed to it. By now on television and especially on social media, I've seen picture after picture, post after post, video after video, article after article—as you probably have too.

When I see an image of a hungry child now, it doesn't burden me as much as before. Why? Because I've become desensitized to it. The image is familiar and not nearly as disturbing unless I pause and remember that this image is of a human being—a real, flesh-and-blood child who is suffering needlessly.

Alongside frequent exposure and the resulting desensitization, our compassion becomes impaired from routinely using social media in a third major way: social media presents its content as if all messages are equal. A tweet from your favorite singer might come in with a text from your grandmother, a newsfeed about some new virus in Africa, and a meeting invitation from your boss. Each message has the same amount of screen real estate, the same kind of structure, even the same colors and fonts. When messages appear this way, our brains can't differentiate between them. What's the most important thing here? Carrie Underwood or Grandma? Ebola or the e-vite?

The messages all look more or less equal. When some new guacamole recipe is followed immediately by an article about a football player who beat up his girlfriend, followed immediately by a funny cat video, followed immediately by an article about an innocent reporter beheaded somewhere in the world, our brains struggle to distinguish which thing is most important. When delicious food is made visually equal to some horrific, murderous crime, our brains register those things as more or less equal, which trains our brains to care less about the bad things.

It's all relative, and it's all out there somewhere in the cyber world. With a quick click, I can ignore it and shop for a new Keurig on Amazon. I don't have to feel my heart ache as I consider the plight of other people dealing with disease, dirty water, terrorism, or abuse. I can read an article about the sequel to my favorite superhero movie instead. Without our even realizing, it happens; we slowly become desensitized over time.

4.4 FROM A DISTANCE

Finally, technology can cause us to care less about others because we don't have to interact directly as often. We can simply text, chat, post, pin, tweet, or blast messages without having to look anyone else in the eye. Even videoconferencing includes the distance of a couple of screens between us and other people.

Let's say you lose your job. You post on Facebook, "Lost my job today." When I see that, what's my most likely course of action? I'll probably comment.

(It's the least I can do.) I'll probably write something like, "Oh, man. Soooo sorry. Praying for you."

On the other hand, let's say we are meeting somewhere for coffee. I see you come in, and I can tell immediately that there's something wrong. We sit down, and you say, "Man, you're not gonna believe what just happened. I just lost my job. I don't even know what happened. What am I gonna tell my wife?"

Together we start talking about what you're going to do. You've got a mortgage. You've got car payments. Your wife was on your insurance, and she has to take expensive prescription medication every day, which your insurance was paying for. You just found out two months ago that one of your kids needs braces. What are you going to do?

My connection to you moves me deep in my heart. When I'm right there in front of you, I care much more than I would from a distance. From afar, it's easier to disconnect, to just walk away, because I don't want to feel the pain. When we're relating face to face with each other in an intimate setting, I'm a participant in what's happening. Across social media, I'm just one more observer, watching as your life drifts by in my feed. When we relate from a distance, we end up caring less.

But why should we care, if no one else does? Because if we have chosen to follow Christ, then we need to understand that God implores us to love others just as he has loved us.

Compassion counts.

4.5 MOVED TO ACTION

The Greek word that the New Testament translates as "compassion" is *splagchnizomai*. It's pronounced "splag-ch-NEE-zo-my." It means "to be moved as to one's bowels." It means to have your bowels yearn. It's a passion arising from a place so deep inside you that you can feel it, that it sounds like your intestines are working, doing something inside of you.

When the New Testament was being written, people believed that love and compassion originated from within your bowels because that was the deepest place in your body, right in your center. When they used the word *splagchnizomai*, they were describing an ache, an empathy for another person felt down deep inside. But even more important, it means that you feel so strongly, *you are moved to action*. Don't miss this. It's powerful. Compassion is not just an emotion, not just some feeling you have that eventually passes.

True compassion demands action.

> **If you say that you care but then don't act on that feeling, it's the same as not caring at all.**

Let me put this another way. If you say that you care but then don't act on that feeling, it's the same as not caring at all. Please reflect on this, because it can be hard to process.

Let's think about what this looks like in our everyday lives. When we see something on Instagram that really connects with us, or something on Facebook that makes us feel some emotion, what do we do? We click. On Instagram, we may spring to double-tap on the picture, because that Likes it. *Tap, tap.* We can see that the person is going through a hard time, and that makes us feel bad for them. So we acknowledge their pain by giving them our Like or double-click. But clicking isn't caring. Truly caring means taking some action. It's getting ourselves involved so we can make a difference in a life. Clicking doesn't change anything. Caring is not Liking a post; it's loving a person.

As you might guess, Jesus is the best example of how this concept is lived out. In every verse in the Gospels where we see Jesus and the word *compassion* together, we immediately see him perform some action. He was there, he felt compassion, and he did something. Every single time.

But don't just take my word for it. Look for yourself. For example, in the gospel of Mark, a man approached Jesus with a desperate need:

"A man with leprosy came and knelt in front of Jesus, begging to be healed. 'If you are willing, you can heal me and make me clean,' he said. *Moved with compassion, Jesus reached out and touched him.* 'I am willing,' he said. 'Be healed!'

Instantly the leprosy disappeared, and the man was healed" (Mark 1:40–42 NLT, emphasis added).

Compassion. *Splagchnizomai.* Jesus felt, and immediately he acted. He touched the man.

Here's another one. When Jesus was leaving Jericho, two blind men heard him going by and called out to him, asking for his help (Matt 20:29–30). "*Jesus had compassion on them and touched their eyes.* Immediately they received their sight and followed him" (Matt. 20:34, emphasis added).

Jesus felt compassion; therefore, he acted. True compassion demands action. To say you care but then not act is not to care at all. We're living in a society where we care less and less about other people. That's even quantifiable: young adults care 40 percent less than they did just a few decades ago. It's tragic. And I believe it's unacceptable for those of us who call ourselves God's people, his church, to just sit by and not act when we're surrounded by people in need.

It boils down to this: the more I obsess over social media, the more I care about me and the less I care about other people. But the more I focus on Jesus—the more I try to get to know him, to serve him, to draw closer to him—the less I care about me and the more I care about his people (John 3:30).

When I look at how Jesus lived his life, and when I allow the words he said to challenge me, something in me changes. I am compelled to deny myself, to take up my cross, and to follow him (Matt. 16:24). I actually *want* to die to myself. I *want* to follow him.

I'm going to ask you some potentially really difficult questions. When was the last time you gave an hour to serve someone else? What about a whole day? Have you ever spent an entire weekend just serving other people?

What about financially? When was the last time you really went out of your way to give financially? I don't mean something obligatory, something people might expect of you. I mean that you gave just because you felt like it. You gave a significant, difficult amount for you that would genuinely make a difference in someone else's life.

When was the last time you missed out on doing something that you really wanted to do because you chose instead to invest that time in someone else? If you've done any of these things recently, then I praise God with you.

If you don't remember the last time you did something like these things, could it be that you're not really that close to Jesus? You might think that's a judgmental question. Possibly. But here's something I know for a fact: when people are really close to Jesus, their lives are no longer about themselves. They become about glorifying God and loving others.

4.6 EXCUSE ME, BUT . . .

Believe it or not, even though I am a pastor, I don't feel like helping other people 24/7. A few years ago I'd been speaking all day at an event in another city. I was exhausted and then I found myself stuck in the Kansas City International Airport late on a Thursday evening, waiting for a long-delayed connecting flight. All I could think about was how tired I was and that I just wanted to get home to my family. I was sitting in one of those uncomfortable airport chairs away from the crowd, just trying to read quietly until the plane was ready.

All of a sudden, a woman was standing in front of me, trying to get my attention. She seemed excited or surprised or something, and she said, "Oh, my goodness! You're my pastor! I can't believe you're here!"

I looked up and forced a smile. I was polite and chatted for a minute, but not much more. After some small talk, she awkwardly said goodbye and walked away slowly. So I raised my book back up and tried to find where I had left off before she interrupted me.

Almost instantly, the reality of that situation hit me. I could feel God's Spirit shaking me out of my selfishness. It was like I could feel him urging me, "What are you doing? Put that book down! We're not done here. Go find that woman and talk to her!"

I closed my book and started looking around for her. Fortunately, she hadn't gone far, and I found her sitting by herself, just kind of staring off into space. As I approached, I could see her mind was somewhere far away, like she was lost in thought.

I cleared my throat, and her face snapped up as she turned to look at me. I said, "Please forgive me. I'm really sorry. But I felt like you wanted to say more." I sat down one chair over from her. "Was there something you wanted to talk about?"

She immediately burst into tears, and her story came gushing out. She told me she was just so ashamed. Through sobs, she explained that she was on a business trip, that she didn't usually drink much alcohol, but that last night she drank way too much. Before I even knew what was happening, she blurted, "And I'm married, and last night I cheated on my husband, and I don't know what I'm going to do."

Not knowing what to say, I started praying silently. Out of the blue I offered, "Well, for whatever it's worth, I think God must really care about you. I don't think it's any coincidence that we just happened to run into each other, here in some airport in a city where neither of us lives. Do you?"

She shook her head. "I guess not. I hope you're right."

I talked with her for a few minutes, then called a counselor I know and put them on the phone together. They made an appointment to meet in person when she got home, and I talked with her for a while longer, probably thirty minutes or so. Finally I told her, "Okay, now this is the hard part. You need to confess this to your husband."

She agreed, and we planned a time when she would do it: 10:00 a.m. on Saturday morning. He was also on a trip, and he'd be home by 10:00 a.m. on Saturday. So that's when she'd tell him. I prayed with her, and I promised I would pray again on Saturday morning and that we'd follow up the week after. We went our separate ways, and I didn't see her again.

A couple of days later, it was Saturday. I hadn't forgotten, but it wasn't like it was at the top of my mind either. My daughter had a dance rehearsal that morning on the other side of town. After dropping her off, I remembered, "Oh, yeah. It's 10:00. Time to pray." Just sitting there in the parking lot in my car, I prayed for the woman and her husband. After a few minutes, I thought, "Well, now I have two hours to kill. What should I do?" So I just started driving around, and the thought suddenly came to me, "Oh, I know . . . I should go to Walmart!" I knew where one was nearby, so I started making my way toward it.

Now, you need to understand: I don't usually go to Walmart, really. I don't enjoy big box stores. I'd rather go to a pet store and look at cats than go to Walmart. It wasn't even like I needed to buy anything. I just couldn't shake this idea that I needed to go to Walmart, so that's what I did. And honestly, even after I walked in, I was kind of just wandering around thinking, "This is so weird. What am I doing at Walmart?"

Then I turned a corner and almost bumped into a guy. We stopped and looked at each other for a split second, like, "Oh, I'm sorry. Excuse me." Then his mouth dropped open, and he blurted, "Oh, my gosh! You're my pastor! I can't believe you're here!"

He burst into tears, grabbed me, leaned his whole weight against me, and started sobbing into my shoulder. Between heaves, he managed to get out, "Thursday night . . . you were in Kansas City . . . in the airport . . . and my wife was there . . . and she confessed to you . . . and she just told me this morning . . . she cheated on me . . . I didn't know what to do . . . so I came to Walmart . . . and now you're here."

When I realized who he was, I was so glad that his wife had interrupted me. I was so glad that now he was interrupting me. I put my arm around him and let him cry. To be honest, I may have cried a little too. Then I said, "Let me ask you something. Do you realize how much God cares about you? Do you realize what he's just done for you? He delayed my flight to get me stuck in the same airport where your wife was so we could have that conversation. Then he sent me here into this Walmart on a Saturday morning as your pastor so I'd be here for you. I don't know what you're going to do. But I *can* tell you this: your marriage must be really important to God. I won't lie to you. It'll be hard. But I believe with all my heart that he wants to heal your marriage, if you'll just let him."

That story still amazes me. The couple went to counseling. He forgave her.

They worked through their differences. God healed their marriage. Let me just tell you again: I am so very thankful to God that he interrupted me.

Don't miss those divine opportunities. I cannot tell you how many times I must have missed them because of my selfishness. I wanted to do what I wanted to do, instead of being open to interruption by the Holy Spirit. I don't know what this looks like for you. Maybe God wants you to pick up the phone and call someone. Maybe when you're driving somewhere, you will see a person with a flat tire, and you will spring into action to help. Whenever you see a need, what will your response be? "This one's mine"? Or "I don't have time for this"? If a person at work is obviously burdened, you can stop to listen, or you can pretend you don't see the need.

Whatever you choose to do, it's completely up to you.

But to say that you care but not act is not to care at all.

Compassion requires action.

4.7 COST OF COMPASSION

Compassion not only requires action, but it also pays a price and sacrifices something. In Luke 10, Jesus tells a compelling story about a man from Samaria who went out of his way to help a Jewish man. In their culture at that time, these two men would most likely have hated each other. But when the Samaritan found the Jewish man beaten up by the side of the road, he put bandages on him, took him to a hotel, and paid two days' worth of his wages to the hotel owner to let the man stay there and to take care of him.

Who would do something like that? Who would spend two days' worth of their own money to take care of a total stranger? Compassion costs, but too often in our culture, we want drive-by compassion. We're willing to do something as long as it's easy for us. As long as it's not too inconvenient.

"I'll click. I'll retweet. I'll Like this. I'll favorite it. I'll share a link." But all of those things are easy. True compassion costs us something.

A few months ago, Amy and I were at a grocery store, and we saw a man and two women, who looked to me like they'd had a hard life, getting some groceries together. I'm not a very touchy-feely kind of person, but when I saw them, I felt moved with compassion deep down inside of me that's hard to explain. I thought to myself, "I feel like we should pay for their groceries."

This is not a normal thing for me. I almost immediately started trying to talk myself out of what I was feeling, arguing with myself about doing something good. "You don't need to pay for their groceries! That's weird! Besides, what if they're insulted?"

I hate to admit it, but I even started testing God. "Okay, God," I prayed. "If they come down the next aisle at the same time I do, I'll buy their groceries."

They did. So I prayed, "Well, just to be sure, God, if when we're in the next aisle, they pick up a box of cereal, then I'll buy their groceries."

And they did. So I pushed through the awkwardness, and I approached them. "I'm sorry. I know this is probably weird, and I really don't want to offend you. But would you let my wife and me pay for your groceries?"

One of the women looked really startled, and I could see a flash of recognition in her face. She said, "Oh, my gosh! Before I went to prison, I used to go to your church." She went on to tell us that she had just been released from prison earlier that day and that she didn't have a place to stay.

In a way, I felt relieved. I thought, "This is perfect. This must be why God prompted me to do this. Two years ago, Amy started a home for women coming out of abusive situations! Here I thought we were supposed to buy this woman groceries, but now I think God actually wants us to help her out with a place to stay. That must be it! Everything's already all set up, so this will be so easy. What a great story!"

I wish I could tell you that's how this situation played out. But it didn't. To protect all of the women at the house, we have rules and specific criteria that each woman has to meet to stay there. Because of this woman's situation, unfortunately, she wasn't eligible. But we weren't willing just to pay for her groceries and then just be done with it. So we referred her to another organization to make sure her immediate needs were met.

What I thought would be a simple, "Oh, here's some money," or, "Of course we have a place where you can stay!" quickly turned into several weeks of working really hard for this woman on a lot of fronts. Things got really complicated really quickly. Compassion costs us something.

As I'm writing this, we don't have a happy ending for her (yet), some clean and tidy resolution. Her story is still unfolding. Clicking is clean. Compassion is messy. It's not always easy and straightforward. Sometimes you think God is leading you one way, but then you discover he is actually doing something else. His way is a lot more interesting. It takes us outside of ourselves, and we learn so much more.

If you're moved to compassion, true compassion, I won't lie to you and tell you it'll be easy and clean. Most likely, it won't be. You'll offer to mentor a child from a hard place, and as you get to know them, you'll start to see how complicated their story is. You might begin serving the youth at your church and realize you

> **Clicking is clean. Compassion is messy.**

have a lot to offer a fifteen-year-old kid—and then find out they're cutting. Things get complicated. Maybe your family will decide to become a foster family. You'll bring a child into your home, fall in love with them, and pour into their life. And they'll get to go home, but you'll have strong suspicions that it's not going to be a stable, healthy situation for them. As your heart breaks, you may wonder if taking care of them even mattered.

When you get outside of yourself, God changes lives. But sometimes he does what you least expect—the life he changes the most is *yours*. We don't have time to take endless selfies and obsess about the wording of our latest brilliant caption when we're caring for someone else. We shouldn't care less than many people used to.

As followers of Jesus, we should care *more*.

Why? Because true compassion demands action. To say you care but not act is not to care at all. Seeing others in need should move us from deep within. And when we feel that compassion, in the name of Jesus we should act.

Chapter 5

REVIVING INTEGRITY

The Struggle with Secret Impurity

Integrity is doing the right thing, knowing no one will know whether you did it or not.

Oprah Winfrey

I never imagined it would happen to me. Sure, I'm like any other guy. I've always been attracted to pretty girls. But I had no idea how this attraction could get so out of control. It started when my big brother got an iPad. He showed me how to remove the "safe search" while looking at images. I started looking at naked celebrities. But once that door was opened, gradually I started watching porn nonstop. Now I'm a junior in college, and I haven't gone a day without looking since I stepped foot on campus. I want to stop, but I don't know if I'll ever be able to.

Brandon J.

As a stay-at-home mother of three, I guess I was overwhelmed and just needed a break. That's not an excuse, but it's the truth. And it wasn't like I was looking at porn or anything. I would just start reading a friend's blog, and then she would mention something on Pinterest, so I'd go look there, then on to some funny cat videos and a new song on another site, which led me to do a little online shopping on Amazon and ordering a present for my sister's birthday. Next thing I knew, three hours had gone by! I thought I'd be online for, like, only ten minutes or so. When I make myself stop and really think about it, this happens several times a week. Which only makes me feel more overwhelmed.

Cindy R.

It started out harmless enough. After our men's Bible study one week, my friend Pete told me about this great gaming site he'd found. I checked it out and liked it because I could play online poker for free. I'm a pretty good player, so one night I got bored and decided to put in my debit card number and maybe win a little. And that first night I won—a lot—more than six hundred dollars! But then a couple of months later, I'd lost it all . . . and more. A lot more. Like over five grand. I haven't told anybody, not even my wife. I never thought of myself as much of a gambler. But now I can't seem to quit. At least not until I can win my money back.

Walter S.

5.1 WHEN NO ONE'S LOOKING

I am living proof that what kids have been saying for generations is true: you'll never again use all the math you learn in high school. Actually, that's not entirely true, because if you have kids of your own, that's when it comes back to bite you. They need help with their homework. Or worse, if you're homeschooling them, you *have* to know what you're talking about. You haven't known panic until your daughter asks you, "Dad, what's the order of operation for a polynomial equation with exponents?"

As tempting as it is to tell my kids to look online or just use their smart phone calculator app, I usually dig in and try to remember Mrs. Simpson's math class from my junior year. It's not that I don't want them to rely on technology to find the answers (isn't that still called cheating?), but I did learn one thing in math early on that stuck with me. And that's the definition of *integer*. You might remember it as well. In math, an integer is simply a whole number, one that can be expressed without a fractional component. The word itself comes from a Latin word that is spelled the same way and means "whole" or "complete."

This is the same root word from which we get *integrity*, an important word that gets thrown around a lot as something everyone wants to have or be known for. However, practicing the habits of integrity—doing the things that keep us whole and completely focused on God—has taken a huge hit, thanks to how much we interact with technology. It's not easy to keep our character healthy and our heart pure when hundreds (if not thousands) of temptations are just a click away.

If integrity is "who you are when no one is looking," then you'll probably agree that it's easier to do the right thing when you know others are watching.

When we believe that no one will know, it's much more tempting to do what we want regardless of what's right. And therein lies one of the biggest challenges with social media and technology.

It's easy to believe that what we do in front of our screens is secret (although it's debatable whether that's really true). After all, if we delete our history, clear our cache, and clean out our cookies, it's easy to believe that no one will ever know what we do online. No one will know what articles we read. What ads we click on. What sites we surf. What videos we watch. Or what pictures we enjoy.

Maybe it's just because I'm a guy, but I immediately think about how technology affects our integrity by tempting us sexually. And while our sexuality is certainly a huge part of our integrity and an issue with which many men struggle (one in two guys have looked at porn today, according to a recent study), I've also realized that our integrity encompasses two other important areas: our convictions and our internal peace. These three areas overlap, as do many personal areas influenced by technology, but it may be helpful to consider each one separately.

Let's start with lust.

5.2 LOOKING, LEARNING, AND LUSTING

When I was a kid, it was difficult to find a picture of a naked woman. To see some skin, you really didn't have many options. If your dad didn't have a secret stash of girlie magazines, your best bet was to have a buddy whose dad did. And that was my path to porn.

In fifth grade, my best friend discovered a big stack of *Playboys* hidden in a trunk with a lock that was supposed to keep out prying eyes. What his dad didn't realize was that virtually no lock on earth can keep out curious eleven-year-old boys. To this day, I remember the rush of curiosity and the thrill of discovery as we turned page after page. I distinctly remember studying

Miss February as if I were cramming for an exam where my very life depend-
ed on remembering every minute detail. For several weeks, my friend and I
spent every possible after-school hour hidden in his closet looking, learning,
and lusting.

This exposure may seem benign by today's standards, but I promise you it
wasn't. Now more than three decades later, if I really try, I can still recall some
of those images that I burned into the hard drive of my brain. Thankfully, besides those hours in my friend's closet with his dad's stash, I saw little growing
up that would further pollute my eager-to-be-tarnished mind. Later when I
was in high school and college, the invention of the VCR (remember those?)
hooked many of my friends into regularly viewing hardcore porn. Somehow
through those years, fortunately, I managed to steer clear of those habits.

It wasn't until after I was married and we got our first internet connection
that I discovered the availability of this once hidden temptation. You might
be too young to remember this, but instead of Wi-Fi, we once used what was
called a "dial-up modem" to access the internet through a phone line. Anyone
who endured this season of technology will never forget the annoying sound
of the modem trying to connect. It was like a rotary dial phone fighting with
a dying cat while aliens shot missiles at a water buffalo scratching its horns on
a chalkboard.

I never will forget the moment I was sitting by my wife, Amy, reading
our first few emails on our free AOL trial account. In total innocence, we
clicked on an email from someone we didn't know. What we saw next was
unlike anything we had ever seen. Even as a pastor with a keen awareness of
the sexual depravity in this world, I was so repulsed by those images that I felt
nauseated. I didn't have the experience to know how to click and delete, so
like a ninja instinctively chopping for the kill, I slapped the power switch and
turned the whole system off.

Suddenly, the virtual world had shifted beneath the weight of that monitor. The device that I had used primarily as a word processor (because for the
most part, that's what PCs were back then) became a new and unexpected

portal to temptation. I mean, if that kind of gross stuff we saw was online, then surely Miss February and her sisters from the rest of the year had to be on there somewhere too.

For the first time in my life, I realized that everything I had ever wanted to see as a curious boy—and everything that I needed to avoid as a Christian—was right there at my fingertips. Again by the grace of God, I learned to set up some systems to shore up my defenses against the temptation. But many (probably even most) of my friends didn't. Images that had once been difficult to find were now constantly within reach.

Just a click away.

5.3 PORN AGAIN

An entire generation has now grown up with easy access to porn. It's as simple to find as a new recipe for enchiladas. You can do your banking online, play games online, read the news online, and research the best hotels in the capital of Algeria. You can also view pornography—unlimited, unfiltered, ungodly images of men and women in graphic situations that make dogs in heat look like a scene from a Jane Austen novel. There's something for virtually every lustful desire, fetish, perversion, or form of sexual attraction.

And an alarming number of people seem to be visiting this online carnal cafeteria to fuel their lustful desires. Studies indicate that 70 percent of men aged eighteen to twenty-four visit porn sites during any given month.[10] Just let that sink in for a moment. Think about the young men you know and care about. Almost three out of four of them are *regularly* consuming a diet of destructive, dehumanizing scenes. We can only imagine how an entire generation's minds are being affected.

For years, people thought porn was strictly a man's problem, but that's clearly no longer the case. Now one in three porn users are women, and they're quickly catching up to the number of male users. According to one source, 34 percent of churchgoing women admit to visiting porn sites online.[11]

If you're reading this book, you might be inclined to share my concern. But if you think I might be overreacting, just consider that the highest percentage of consumers of pornography are children aged twelve to seventeen.[12] And these kids aren't just viewing; more than one in five teenage girls say they have posted nude or seminude photos of themselves online. These numbers don't even scratch the surface of what's happening on services like Snapchat and Tumblr.

As if all this weren't enough, it's not just looking and lusting that is getting people into trouble. Simply connecting, or reconnecting, with new friends or old flames through social media is a massive source of temptation for many. More and more studies are correlating the use of social media with higher rates of marital infidelity.

Here is some of the evidence:

> Previous studies also support the conclusion that there's a connection between social networking and marital problems. Adjusting for other variables, 32 percent of heavy social-media users say they've thought seriously about leaving their spouse, compared with 16 percent of people who don't use social networks, according to a 2011 University of Texas at Austin survey of 1,600 married 18- to 39-year-olds. This is one of the few—if not only—publicly available representative surveys in the U.S. that contains questions about both social-network use and indicators of marriage well-being, Valenzuela adds. One-third of divorce filings in the U.K. contain the word Facebook, a separate 2011 survey by Divorce Online, a legal services website, found.[13]

It would be unfair to blame Facebook and other social media sites or technology for adulterous affairs. Facebook doesn't make people cheat. People decide to cheat. But we have access to many opportunities online that—without accountability—can turn technological blessings into curses.

5.4 ONLY LOOKING

When I first started writing Christian books, I wouldn't have bothered to waste words explaining why looking lustfully at erotic images is wrong. Almost everyone pursuing God would have agreed that looking at images or videos that stir lustful thoughts or actions is unquestionably immoral.

Not so today.

Which brings me to the second point of attack on our integrity. Over time and with repeated use, technology is eroding both our moral beliefs and our commitment to acting on what we believe. According to one study, "Roughly two-thirds (67 percent) of young adult men and one-half (49 percent) of young adult women now believe that viewing pornography is acceptable."[14] In one short decade, the standards of what is perceived as right and wrong have unequivocally changed, perhaps faster than any other time in history. Now even faithful church attenders push back and ask, "What's the big deal if I look? It's no one else's business. I'm not hurting anyone." Some Christians have even asked me, "Isn't looking at porn better than going out and sinning with another person?"

> **Over time and with repeated use, technology is eroding both our moral beliefs and our commitment to acting on what we believe.**

No. Sin is sin, whether it happens in our minds, in our hearts, or by using our bodies. Obviously, the consequences of our sin vary according to the actions. But many people are convincing themselves that looking at porn has no consequences and doesn't hurt anyone else. But that's simply not true. What used to be considered wrong has gradually become tolerated and eventually simply accepted by many, if not most.

For example, I clicked on a news link from a tweet earlier today to read about a crisis in the Middle East. At the bottom of the page were ads for other, unrelated articles you could click on and read. To be honest, the images didn't shock me. I see similar ads several times a week on similar, respected news sites. But what has become normal, if viewed from a distance, is anything but normal. Right there in front of me was a barely dressed blond woman. She managed to cover the parts that would make the picture unacceptable while accentuating the features that were certain to draw attention. Right next to that image was a naked couple in bed. Sure, their "essentials" were carefully (although barely) covered by the sheets, but there wasn't much left to the imagination. The article, if you could call it that, was seductively entitled, "Seven Ways to Drive Your Lover Mad in Bed." (Notice that it promises seven ways to please not your *spouse* but your "lover.")

Times have changed.

But that doesn't mean morality should. While all this sexy stuff may be normal, that doesn't make it right. No matter how much our culture tries to normalize what God calls sin, becoming "normal" doesn't make wrong right. The apostle Paul says it directly: "But among you there must *not be even a hint* of sexual immorality, or of any kind of impurity, or of greed, because these are improper for God's holy people" (Eph. 5:3, emphasis added). Not even a hint!

I'm sure you know what a hint is, but let's play a little game. I'll give you some examples, and you tell me if they include a hint of sexual immorality. We'll start with easy questions and move on to less obvious ones.

If someone posts a sexually explicit picture, is this a hint of immorality?

Of course it is. But that one's too easy.

What about a suggestive ad with an image of a barely dressed person? Hint or not?

Years ago, teenage boys from my youth group confessed that they lusted after department store newspaper ads of models wearing bras and panties. If those can create lust, surely more suggestive ads will, if not more.

What about a raunchy tweet or dirty joke posted on Facebook?

Again, to God, that would qualify as more than a hint.

How about pinning a nearly nude Ryan Gosling meme on Pinterest?

No matter how good he looks, that still would fall squarely into God's inappropriate zone.

You might be tempted to write me off as a religious fuddy-duddy. That's totally fine. If you don't strive to know and follow Jesus, then fair enough; that's your choice. But if you want to live in a way that honors our Savior—if you want to follow Jesus in a sin-saturated, selfie-centered world—then you will have to be different.

Seriously. Not even a hint.

Our convictions must be guided by God's timeless principles, not by the ever-eroding popular opinion on whatever happens to be acceptable now. We must stand firm in our faith, fighting the battle against the temptations and sinful habits that our enemy gladly uses to pull us away from knowing God and loving others. If we want our hearts to remain intact and whole, not stained by lust and haunted by impure images, then we must set limits on what we access with technology.

This may sound unlikely at best or impossible at worst. But I want to encourage you to believe that God wouldn't ask you to do something without giving you the power to do it. If you are #struggling right now in this area, whether seriously or occasionally, or if you just want to better purify your use of technology, keep reading.

With God all things are possible, and he gives the power to swim against the cultural current of our hyper-sexualized society.

5.5 PLEASANT BOUNDARIES

If we're going to follow Christ with integrity, we must use technology wisely. The Bible is more than clear that we are deceiving ourselves if we think we can flirt with lust and not contribute to our soul's destruction. Solomon, the wisest man who ever lived, warned his son of the temptation of following the wrong type of woman, "Keep to a path far from her, do not go near the door of her house" (Prov. 5:8).

Notice he didn't say, "You can look, but don't touch." Or, "Here, son, make sure you wear protection." No! Solomon essentially shouted, "Are you crazy?!

Stay away! Don't even get close to the edge of sin!" Oddly, in our culture, many people want to do just the opposite, to see how close they can get to trouble without crossing the line. But God's Word teaches us to stay as far away from temptation as possible.

I love the way David phrases this idea in Psalm 16:6: "The boundary lines have fallen for me in pleasant places." God has put some fences or boundaries in place, and I'm very thankful he has. The fences keep the good stuff in and the bad stuff out. His boundaries are designed not to confine me but to protect me.

Think about it. Most people I know don't plan to ruin their lives. I don't know anyone who thinks, "If I can connect with an old boyfriend on Facebook, I can totally wreck my life. I can almost guarantee an ugly divorce full of expensive lawyers helping us fight over custody rights for the kids. I can devastate my husband and drop a nuclear bomb of pain into my kids' lives. And I can spend the next years of my life trying to forgive myself, rebuild my life, and regain my name." No one plans like that, but these things happen *every day*.

Same with pornography. I don't know a single man who wanted to crush the wife he loves when she discovered his "little secret." But one glance followed by another click often leads to an addiction that seems impossible to overcome.

So if you're going to love God with all of your heart, mind, and soul, you will have to be deliberate about protecting your heart, mind, and soul. To follow Jesus in this selfie-centered, lust-filled world, you'll be wise to set up some online boundaries to keep you safe. Before temptation can reach you, find ways to push it farther away.

I'm far from perfect, but let me share with you the defenses I have set up to keep me safe. These safeguards are pleasant boundaries to me. Instead of hoping I have the strength to get out of trouble when temptation knocks, I've decided to do my best to keep temptation from ever getting close to my front door. As I tell you what I do, remember these are for me.

Knowing my weaknesses and vulnerabilities, I've decided to eliminate all temptation (I can think of) on my computer by using tracking software that sends a detailed (and scored) list of every single click I make.

Every single click.

This software sends a weekly report to two different men, both of whom have the authority to remove me from my role as pastor. If I didn't have this boundary in place, there might be times I'd find myself vulnerable. But it's been too many years to count since I've been vulnerable on a computer, because years ago I shut that door. Slammed it. Nailed it. Bolted it shut. Now that I have no access, I'm never tempted. I no longer have the option to jump over the edge into an abyss that would wreck my heart, destroy my marriage, and undermine my calling. These are three of the many reasons this boundary is pleasant, necessary, and freeing to me.

5.6 #GETHONESTWITHYOURSELF

Now that I've been open with you, it's your turn. To help with the process, I'll ask you some questions. To increase your odds of living with online integrity, you must start by telling the truth.

Where are you weak?

Where are you vulnerable?

When are you most likely to get caught in a trap that could destroy what you treasure most?

Now is an important moment. Be truthful.

You are only as strong as you are honest.

I want you to pause for a moment and think

You are only as strong as you are honest.

about when you are the most vulnerable. Maybe it's when you travel. You're away from home. Working hard. Feeling lonely. And temptation strikes. Perhaps it's when you're bored. Without much happening on a Sunday afternoon, your mind starts to wander. You're playing on social media. A few clicks later, you can end up somewhere you shouldn't be.

Maybe you're easily distracted when you're angry, anxious, or overwhelmed. When you're not feeling good about things, you may realize you're more vulnerable than in your healthier moments. You may be tempted by trouble when your spouse is out of town. You don't have as much to do, and trouble seems to find you. Or perhaps you're vulnerable when you're looking for something to watch on Netflix or are "innocently" browsing Instagram. You start out well but end up bad—again.

Maybe it's gotten even worse for you. Perhaps you crossed some lower barriers a long time ago, and now you're looking almost daily at things that are dangerous to your faith and poisonous to your soul. Maybe you've sent or received inappropriate pics or texts.

Be honest.

You are only as strong as you are honest.

Once you've determined your most vulnerable points, you'll want to put up boundaries. If you don't have a strong wall of defense, build one. If you have some vulnerable spots in what used to be a wall, close those gaps and eliminate the obvious access points. If you are even remotely tempted or think you might be vulnerable, plan today to stay out of trouble tomorrow.

Chances are you might not be tempted by everything I've suggested. But if you're interested in finding out how to set up safeguards of your own, please review appendix 2 at the end of this book. You might already know other ways to protect yourself from troubling habits or inclinations. Be honest with yourself, and do everything you can to put protective measures in place. If you might be tempted to watch questionable YouTube videos, delete the app. If your device won't let you delete it, use a locking app with a code that only one of your accountability partners has. No parody vlog or cat video is worth being vulnerable. If you're constantly getting into trouble on your smart TV, find appropriate ways to block the source. But if you can't, trade in your smart device for a dumb one.

Yes, I'm dead serious.

Same with social media. If you find yourself revisiting people, sites, pictures or videos that hurt your relationship with God, the purity of your mind, and the intimacy between you and your spouse (or future spouse), drop that social media. Before you slam this book down (or delete the iBook) and start tweeting hateful things about me, pause and give what I am saying some thought. If you aren't a Christian, you don't have to worry about anything here. But if you truly want to honor God, living by his Holy Spirit to avoid even a *hint* of sexual immorality, then lose it.

Believe it or not, people before us lived for centuries without the ability to spray their thoughts in 140 characters or less to a group of people who are barely paying attention anyway because they're more concerned about what *they're* going to say next. No retweets, comments, or Likes are worth the poison that will contaminate your soul and hurt your relationships with the people you love the most.

Not even a hint.

But let's not stop there. Since we're going crazy in pursuing online purity, if you're married, let me suggest that you give your spouse access to all your passwords. After all, we shouldn't have any secrets from our spouse, should we? If we have nothing to hide, why not give him or her full access? Or better yet, you might even consider sharing accounts when possible. I know many couples who have a shared Facebook account and love that they never have to worry about what their loved one is doing or saying.

You might make some personal rules as well. Maybe you won't text or direct message the opposite sex unless it's mandatory for business purposes. Or under no circumstances will you share personal information or imply anything that would be questionable.

So give it some thought. Where are you weak or vulnerable? And what are you going to do about it?

5.7 THE PRICE OF PEACE

When you think about it, no one stumbles into righteousness. People fall into sin every day. But no one just falls into holiness. It requires making deliberate, prayerful choices and walking an intentional path. Which brings us to the third stress point where technology often destroys our integrity: it robs us of our peace.

Peace is a funny thing. We tend to think of it as the absence of conflict, the period between wars and military battles where opposing sides at least pretend to get along. (Does that remind you of some marriages?) Whether it's the "peace and quiet" longed for by a stay-at-home mom with young children or something negotiated among world political leaders, we all tend to think of peace as this quiet, calm, serene state of being.

But in the Jewish culture, the word for peace, *shalom*, has a much richer, fuller meaning than just "getting along" with everyone. In fact, shalom is one of the underlying principles of the Torah, the first five books of the Bible that Jews consider foundational to their history. Shalom means not only the kind of personal peace we often crave but also a harmonious environment and a sense that everything's right with the world.

> People fall into sin every day. But no one just falls into holiness.

Shalom is about living out the fullness of who God created you to be and enjoying the abundance of blessings God showers on you. This kind of peace includes a feeling of confidence and blessing because you know who you are and what you're supposed to be doing. It also encompasses a sense of security, an ability to relax and not have to try to control everything because you're able to trust in God's goodness as well as his plan. What's interesting is that peace, *shalom*, cannot be earned like a paycheck after a week's work. It comes as a free gift if we're just willing to receive it.

We all say we want more peace, but I wonder if we recognize what we do that often robs us of God-given peace. Like checking our email obsessively because we're afraid we'll miss something, when we could be enjoying time with God, our family, or a close friend we've been missing. Or like responding to email to make sure everyone views us as the hardworking, superefficient people we are, when we should be focusing on more important priorities. Like killing time surfing for an hour or so because we are avoiding a difficult conversation. Like obsessing over the latest hot app game when we should be playing with our kids. Like numbing the pain in our life by clicking to the "wrong sites" for a lustful escape from reality.

Here's what many people miss: when we misuse technology, we're robbing ourselves of the peace we so desperately crave, because even the momentary escape is followed by waves of intense guilt. We want to numb the pain, but on the other side of our binge, the pain is still there, only worse. We love the momentary distraction, but then reality screams at us and our responsibilities pile up. We love the thrill of the lust, but the fear of getting caught haunts us and robs us of sleep and peace. Like a person dying of thirst who gulps salt water, that which is supposed to satisfy only intensifies our need. So life goes on as usual. More stress. More anxiety. More worries.

And less peace.

Everyone talks about being so busy and longing for more rest, but not many of us are willing to guard our integrity by unplugging and protecting our personal peace.

One way to measure the peace in your life is to think about your level of satisfaction and contentment. Are you always striving for more, trying to keep up with your Facebook friends and Twitter followers? Or can you appreciate the enormous blessings you've enjoyed today—a bed to sleep in, food to eat, a family to love, friends to enjoy, a car to drive, and a job that provides income?

I'm convinced that our peace (or the absence thereof) is directly tied to what we focus on each day. We don't need a lot of specialized knowledge or superhuman will to achieve peace. We simply need to keep paying attention to what we are doing with our time. If we're focused on escaping the pain of life, avoiding problems, and trying to control our image to the rest of the world, then we won't have much peace. And the more we seek to surf porn, feed a shopping or gambling addiction online, or envy others for all they appear to have online, the more miserable, restless, and anxious we're going to feel.

Guaranteed.

The Bible is quite clear about how we can cultivate and enjoy God's peace, as well as how we can lose it. When we worry and fret over what we don't have, what we wish we had, what someone else thinks of us, or how jealous we are of others, inner peace remains elusive. Scripture tells us, "Worry weighs a person down; an encouraging word cheers a person up" (Prov. 12:25 NLT).

Whenever technology increases our worry, whenever it helps us fragment our attention and compartmentalize our hearts, it also kills our peace. We worry when we rely on our own abilities rather than trust in God. But his Word tells us, "Do not be anxious about anything, but in every situation, by prayer and petition, with thanksgiving, present your requests to God. And the peace of God, which transcends all understanding, will guard your hearts and your minds in Christ Jesus" (Phil. 4:6–7).

When we lack peace, we live stressed and afraid. We're always wondering when the next problem is going to pop up, the next conflict arise, the next crisis hit. Even when things are good, we hold our breath, constantly expecting that other shoe to drop. (It always does, right?) It's hard to be whole-hearted in our pursuit of God when our thoughts are polluted by worry and anxiety. Instead, we should, "Let the peace of Christ rule in your hearts, since as members of one body you were called to peace. And be thankful" (Col. 3:15).

Now is a great time to be brutally honest.

Are you addicted to something online? Looking lustfully? Spending uncontrollably? Surfing endlessly? Playing continually? Gambling consistently? Scrolling incessantly?

Tell the truth.

While it's never going to be fun or easy to kick an online addiction, you'll be surprised how quickly your peace will be restored once you surrender the

It's hard to be whole-hearted in your pursuit of God when your thoughts are polluted by worry and anxiety.

problem to God. Because if you're serious about pursuing God's healing, he'll meet you wherever you are.

So if you find yourself overwhelmed with virtual temptation, remember that God isn't surprised. He knows what you face, and he's already made a plan to help you find freedom. Paul offers us this amazing promise: "No temptation has overtaken you except what is common to mankind. And God is faithful; he will not let you be tempted beyond what you can bear. But when you are tempted, he will also provide a way out so that you can endure it" (1 Cor. 10:13). Don't miss the power of these words.

God will provide a way out.

What's your way out? I don't know. It could be something dramatic. But be honest. You are a sharp person. If some small tweak would have fixed your problem, you would have done it a long time ago.

Your way out might be confessing to your spouse, your best friend, your small group, or your pastor. It might be deleting an app and making sure you can't get to it again. You might need to lock down your phone, iPad, iPod, Kindle, computer, TV, and anything else so you can't get to anything you shouldn't see. I don't know what you need to do. But chances are you have a pretty good idea.

God promises to give you a way out.

James tells us, "Submit yourselves, then, to God. Resist the devil, and he will flee from you. Come near to God and he will come near to you" (James 4:7–8).

If you want to be a man or woman of integrity, then maybe it's time for you to submit to God like never before. That's where you start. Then with Christ's power, you can resist the devil and all his e-temptations. Tragically, so many people do just the opposite. They resist God's promptings and give in to the temptations of the evil one. But that won't be you. And it won't be me.

Instead, we will live with online integrity. Because our lives are not about us. We will not gratify the self-centered lusts of our flesh because we're born of the Spirit. We will not allow God's loving truth to slide into the quicksand of popular opinion and sink us into lower standards. We will guard our peace. We won't allow how we use tech to rob us of our purpose, passion, and power.

As we pray, God will give us wisdom to set up pleasant boundaries and safeguards to keep temptation as far away from us as possible. And when we are tempted, we know that Jesus has already given us an escape route.

We will seek him, see his way out, and take it.

We have his power to overcome sin. We have his Spirit to lead us into righteousness. We have his presence to keep us pure.

We will be whole.

We will be complete.

We will know the peace of the Lord.

Chapter 6

REMEMBERING ENCOURAGEMENT

The Struggle with Constant Criticism

Any fool can criticize, condemn, and complain, but it takes character and self-control to be understanding and forgiving.

Dale Carnegie

I don't know why I let it get to me, but I do. I just can't stand to see immoral behavior accepted like it's no big deal. So I find myself always leaving snarky comments and critical observations about all kinds of political, social, and spiritual issues—everything from gun control and abortion to the latest celebrity coming out. Since I don't have to sign my name, just my username, I feel free to be harsh, judgmental, and outright mean sometimes. I don't think God approves of some of the comments I've made on various sites and blog posts. But for some reason, I just keep posting them.

Tim P.

It's just a little blog I do on fashion, makeup, accessories—you know, girl stuff. But lately it seems that no matter what I post, I get slammed for being too trendy or too old school, too young and junior-ish, or too old and matronly. One commenter in particular, luvzshoes261, loves putting me down. I tried responding at first and asking her if we could have an offline conversation, but she ignored my requests. I think she just enjoys the attention that comes from being a constant critic. I know I shouldn't be so sensitive, but I just can't take it anymore. I don't see any other option besides quitting my blog.

Amanda B.

As a young pastor of a growing church, I know we have to have a website and use the many benefits of social media. But I get so tired of all the anonymous critics who feel "led by the Lord" to share their latest "concern" about our church. Some comment on the song selections while others slam my sermon that week. Some want more community groups and others want Sunday school instead. There's no way everyone can agree on what our church should be. But honestly, if I could, I'd love to shut down our site and social media—or else figure out a way to make critics identify themselves.

Jerry W.

6.1 OUT THERE FOREVER

On September 7, 2012, a young teen posted a chilling nine-minute video on YouTube called *Amanda Todd's Story: Struggling, Bullying, Suicide, Self Harm.* In the video this shy, vulnerable girl slowly flips through handwritten note cards detailing the pain she'd endured after trusting someone she met on Facebook. Amanda's story started innocently enough, but then they always do, right?

A curious seventh-grade girl met a nice and flattering guy online. Amanda's newfound Facebook friend was charming and knew exactly what to say to flatter her young heart. He poured out generous compliments, telling her nonstop just how beautiful she was to him. After slowly winning her over, he started making demands. For a year, the man begged Amanda to flash him her bare chest. Since she trusted the guy and enjoyed his attention, she finally and reluctantly gave in.

Amanda could never imagine how much that one decision would hurt.

Sometime later, Amanda started receiving threats from her "friend" to put on a show, or her topless picture would go online for the whole world to see. Her friends. Her parents. Her teachers. Everyone would see her if she didn't agree to his requests. On Christmas break in 2010, the police came to her home at 4:00 a.m. with the bad news. The nude picture was public, now circulating freely on the internet and gaining momentum by the minute. Amanda's worst nightmare had come true. And this was only the beginning. You can imagine how she was ridiculed at school. Friends turned on her. Rumors flew. Guys pointed and whispered. Shamed and seeing no way to escape, young Amanda started dying a slow, agonizing death inside.

In her now famous YouTube clip (that to date has received more than 19 million views), Amanda held up a notecard that symbolized what the finality of her mistake felt like. It read, "I can never get that photo back. It's out there forever." Because Amanda was hopeless and depressed, her family moved her to a new home and school, hoping she could start over and make new friends. But her past wouldn't go away. To cope, she started cutting herself and turned to drugs and alcohol, which only made things worse. Anxiety, depression, and panic set in. One year later, the same man started a Facebook page using Amanda's humiliating photo as his profile picture. To add insult to injury, he contacted her new friends, and before long, everyone at her new school was aware of the page and her past.

Still longing for a safe harbor, Amanda's family moved her to yet another school. But each time she moved to a new school, a new Facebook page would emerge with her embarrassing decision displayed for the world to see. After reconnecting with an "old guy-friend," she had sex with him on a school break even though he had a girlfriend. Amanda really believed this guy liked her. She didn't realize he wanted only one thing from her.

The following week, this guy's girlfriend and about fifteen others confronted Amanda, shouting profanities and insults at her in front of a much larger crowd. Kids shouted, "Look around! Nobody likes you!" among many other insults I won't put in print. Finally someone called out, "Just punch her already!" That's when the beating began. Students captured the punishment on camera phones to immortalize the stomping. Once the mob finished what they came to do, the severely wounded Amanda made her way to the safety of a secluded ditch where she stayed until her father found her.

This was more than Amanda could handle. Hoping to end the pain, she drank bleach in an effort to end her life. Thankfully, paramedics were able to get her to the hospital and save her life by pumping her stomach. Although they successfully removed the poison from her body, they couldn't clean the insults from her heart. Cruel students posted online, "She deserved it. I hope she's dead." Others recommended she try a different kind of bleach and made taunts like, "I hope she dies next time."

As the music plays in the background of Amanda's sobering video, time moves slowly. Her face is almost invisible in the distance. One by one she flips through the cards revealing chapter after chapter of her painful story. She admits that she made mistakes. There is no doubt about that. But she didn't deserve to be bullied, criticized, and publicly shamed. The last two cards read: "I have nobody. I need someone. [sad face] My name is Amanda Todd."

And the video ends.

On October 10, just over one month after Amanda posted her video, she took her life.

6.2 SAY IT TO MY FACE

Unfortunately, Amanda's story is not rare. More and more people are falling victim to cyber bullying. The most recent studies show that *more than half* of all young people using social media have been bullied. And a shocking 95 percent of young people who have either experienced or witnessed bullying acknowledge that they and others have done nothing about it.[15]

Think about it. For the first time in history, people can virtually say anything they want about someone else. It's immediate, it's permanent, and it's anonymous. Every day, people tweet under the cover of a fake name or dummy account, and they can do the same on most forms of social media. There's zero accountability. Telling the truth doesn't matter to some people. Making others look bad, taking cheap shots, and creating controversy draws attention to these anonymous critics. But what may seem like harmless fun to the person making the post can be devastating on the other end of the conversation.

Have you ever read the comments on an online news story? Any hater with a computer or phone has the freedom to show publicly just how foolish they are, and so they do! It's almost like comment posting exists for dysfunctional, miserable people to vent their opinions about *anything:* the story, the author, the subject of the story, the content of other people's comments, or even what the poster ate for breakfast. You can freely spout off, and no one knows or has to know who you are.

The Tonight Show host Jimmy Fallon recently produced a revealing video about major league baseball player Robinson Cano. Cano used to play for the New York Yankees before signing a huge, ten-year contract to play second base for the Seattle Mariners. Since New Yorkers were mad about Cano deserting their team, Fallon gave individuals a chance to shout at a giant picture of the ball player, and he captured everything on video. Several people passionately booed at the picture, even shouting rude comments to their once beloved hero.

What these critical fans didn't know was that Cano was actually there, standing right behind his picture! Whenever they began loudly expressing their disapproval of him, Cano stepped out and greeted them. And every time, the person would be embarrassed. Most smiled and apologized profusely, explaining that they were only joking and were really honored to meet him. We can't help but laugh watching this perfect illustration of people saying ridiculous things that they would never have the courage to say to someone's face. So much of the criticism people hurl today is anonymous, or at least done from a distance, that it can be hard for them to realize its impact.

Chances are good that you will be tempted to join the critical party. When another football player gets arrested, you can toss in your two cents about his crime. Or when a female celebrity dresses provocatively for the latest award ceremony, you can tell the world what you think of her gown. If a famous pastor makes a mistake, you can tell everyone you know what you think about it in 140 characters or less.

Or you can choose to be quiet.

Just because you *can* do something doesn't mean you should. Although sharing your opinion can be important—and even sometimes helpful—much of what happens online is just plain, old-fashioned gossip.

Just because you *can* do something doesn't mean you should.

And because anyone can say anything, it's important to remember that not everything you see online is true. Were you one of the nine million viewers in one week to see the YouTube video of the young woman who captured her own upside-down twerking fail? After shaking it while doing a handstand, she fell onto her coffee table and ignited a small house fire. But this amazing fail was actually a stunt planned by another late night television host, Jimmy Kimmel, to see how far the joke would fly.

Or maybe you believed waitress Dayna Morales in New Jersey when she posted a picture on Facebook of a $93.55 restaurant tab and claimed her customer wouldn't tip and left a note mocking her sexual orientation by saying, "I'm sorry but I cannot tip because I don't agree with your lifestyle and how you live your life." The post went viral. People were understandably outraged, venting their feelings on every forum possible, and many even sent Morales money to express their support.

Problem is the story wasn't true. The customers in question were outraged by the claim and provided a New York news group with a copy of their $93.55 receipt, printed the same time as the one Morales photographed for Facebook, showing an $18.00 tip.[16]

Or maybe you really thought Paris Hilton tweeted, "RIP Nelson Mandela. Your 'I have a dream speech' was so inspiring." Even Paris knows better—after all, everyone knows Jackie Robinson gave that famous speech. (Okay, just checking to see if you were paying attention. Yes, I know it was Martin Luther King Jr.)

Maybe before we talk about how we should handle some inevitable online challenges, we should first make sure we're not contributing to the problem.

6.3 HEY, HAVE YOU HEARD . . .

I heard someone say, "I hate when people gossip about me. That's why I almost never gossip about anything unless it's really important. And then I tell only a few people." It's funny, but this statement accurately reflects many views on gossip:

1. "I know it's wrong."
2. "I hate it when people gossip about me."
3. "But it doesn't really keep me from gossiping about others."

Just so we're clear, let's define gossip and what God thinks about it. Rick Warren says, "When we are talking about a situation with somebody who is neither part of the problem or part of the solution, then we are probably gossiping." Before you tweet your opinion, share a link, or post a comment, it is wise to ask yourself, "Am I helping, or am I simply gossiping?" Because God is crystal clear on how he feels about gossip. Solomon said, "There are six things the Lord hates, seven that are detestable to him . . . a false witness who pours out lies and a person who stirs up conflict in the community" (Prov. 6:16, 19).

What a perfect way to describe a gossip: "a false witness who pours out lies," and someone who "stirs up conflict in the community." God hates that. If you're a parent, you know how upset you get if someone says something untrue about one of your kids. Well, each time you gossip about someone else, you're spreading rumors about one of God's children. And he's a loving Father who absolutely hates gossip.

Oddly enough, there's something sickeningly attractive about the sin of gossip. It intrigues us, draws us, lures us. I admit a while back, when some pastor got caught in an online skirmish, I'd follow the tweets and search the hashtags to see what everyone was saying about it. Although I wasn't participating in sharing the news, I *was* participating: by spectating. Proverbs describes this strange satisfaction so well: "The words of a gossip are like choice morsels; they go down to the inmost parts" (Prov. 18:8).

If sharing or reading online gossip is an area of struggles for you, let's be honest about why you're drawn to it. Ask yourself and answer truthfully: Why do you participate in gossip? What draws you? Why are you tempted by it? What's the reward you get from participating in gossip? What's the payoff?

You might be like a lot of people. Knowing something juicy makes us feel important, like an insider who's "in the know." Sometimes we honestly enjoy hearing the dirt. Maybe it vindicates some secret suspicion we have always had, prompting us to think, "I knew there was something not quite right about them. I never really trusted them. This doesn't surprise me at all."

Then there's the part of us that feels curiously relieved and a little superior when someone else looks bad. We may have our issues, but at least we haven't done what *they* did. Why do we feel better when someone else looks bad? If we take it to a deeper level, I believe we will find that some of us search the net for dirt because we are dissatisfied with our own lives. Since we're miserable, we enjoy seeing someone else suffer. I really believe this behavior is a reflection of the depths of our sinful human hearts.

But finding joy in the suffering of others is not how God made us. We're better than that.

6.4 #MAKESMECRAZY

The people being gossiped about hate it, and God hates it. So before you post, comment, or link, consider three sets of questions to keep yourself gossip-free online.

Before you comment on anything online, ask yourself the first set of questions: "Is what I'm about to say helpful or hurtful? Will this build others up or tear them down? What's my intention behind what I'm about to type?"

Paul surely never dreamed of the technological advances we have today. But he still directly addressed our tendency to gossip: "Do not let any unwholesome talk come out of your mouths, but only what is helpful for building others up according to their needs, that it may benefit those who listen" (Eph. 4:29). If what you intend to communicate is unwholesome, don't type it. Don't tweet it. Don't post it. As followers of Jesus, we want everything we say to build up others. The Bible tells us, "A scoundrel

> If what you intend to communicate is unwholesome, don't post it. As followers of Jesus, we want everything we say to build up others.

plots evil, and on their lips it is like a scorching fire. A perverse person stirs up conflict, and *a gossip separates close friends*" (Prov. 16:27–28, emphasis added).

We all hate when others gossip about us or someone we love, but we don't always realize how quickly we can fall into gossiping ourselves. Sometimes we even think we're being honest, but actually we're disguising a dig. You know what I'm talking about. We start with something positive before sharing what we really think—the proverbial turd rolled in glitter.

- "I've always liked this restaurant, except for the poor service last time."
- "She's always been someone I've admired, but after what she said last week . . ."
- "For years I've really respected him. But let me tell you what I just found out."

Even Christians fall prey to deceiving ourselves in fairly elaborate ways. When I was a new Christian in college, I never wanted to miss the Thursday evening prayer meeting because if you did, you were fair game. "We need to pray for Craig," other Christians would say. "He doesn't seem as passionate about God as he used to be. If he was, he'd be here praying with us. And did you hear that he said another bad word during practice? Yep, we definitely need to pray for him." One time they were praying in my living room, and I had a test early the next morning. About 11:00 p.m., I told them I was going to bed. I actually heard one guy tell the group they needed to pray for me because I cared more about my class than I did about God's presence. #MakesMeCrazy!

Now in that same spirit of carefully disguising gossip as well-intentioned prayer requests, many make their "concerns" public on Facebook or some other form of social media. We've all heard or seen these kinds of prayers, if we have not been the person praying them.

- "Please be in prayer for Megan. She's doing things with her boyfriend she shouldn't be doing."
- "Pray that Bob stays away from that woman in accounting who keeps flirting with him."
- "Hey, y'all, lift up Jenn in prayer NOW!! She was boozin @ the party last nite."
- "My dad lost his cool again with mom. Believe with me that God will do a work in him."

While it's always good to pray, not all prayer requests belong online. At least not with the kinds of descriptions that imply something you may know very little about in someone else's life. If you're going to request prayer online, do it in a way that doesn't make others look bad.

Maybe you're inclined to push back and argue, "But, Craig, it's okay to talk about things if they're true, right?" Not necessarily. Everything you say should be true, but not everything that's true should be said. Before you type it, ask yourself, "Is this helpful? Or hurtful?"

If it's not helpful, don't say it.

6.5 INITIAL PUBLIC OFFERING

The second set of questions you should ask yourself to avoid gossiping online are equally important. Before sharing your thoughts, ask yourself, "Am I making private matters public? Am I about to share something that would be better handled privately?" In his wisdom, Solomon said, "It is foolish to belittle one's neighbor; a sensible person keeps quiet. A gossip *goes around telling secrets,* but those who are trustworthy can keep a confidence" (Prov. 11:12–13 NLT, emphasis added).

If you share what should be secret, you're gossiping. I'll never forget what happened when a group of well-intentioned Christians made a horrible mistake in misusing social media. Amy and I were working with a couple to heal their marriage. Earlier in the year, the husband confessed to committing adultery. As painful as that was for his wife, she wanted to save their marriage and was seeking God to help her forgive her husband.

Thankfully, we were able to make considerable progress with this couple. Not only had the husband repented of his sins, but with God's help he was improving in several other ways that demonstrated his love for his wife. She was beginning to be responsive to him, and their marriage was definitely moving in the right direction. I've learned from counselors that at some point in the healing process, it's wise to bring in others for support. If a couple keeps their struggles totally private, it's hard for them to heal. Opening up to trusted friends for prayer and accountability is often a key element in their healing. So we all agreed that this couple would share their situation with their small group at church for prayer and support.

As the husband explained what he had done, tears streamed down his face. His wife graciously reached over and grabbed his hand to show him (and the others) that she loved him, supported him, and forgave him. I remember thinking when I saw that gesture, "This marriage is going to make it," and the rest of the meeting was more powerful than I can describe. Another couple opened up and said they had been through the same thing and explained how God healed their marriage. There wasn't a dry eye in the house. Everyone prayed. Everyone hugged. And everyone went home a little closer to each other and to God.

God was doing one of the things he does best: restoring the brokenhearted and bringing healing. But one woman in the group did something we had asked everyone *not* to do. Whenever you trust a group with this kind of sensitive information, you must always tell them to keep it strictly confidential. No one tells anyone. Not a soul. That's the rule. Sadly, this woman decided to tell "just one friend." And that one friend decided to post the information on Facebook, saying, "Please pray for _____," with the couple's names in the blank. She went on to explain that the husband had an affair with his assistant, and she wanted everyone to pray for their marriage.

Unfortunately, this couple trying to heal was devastated—especially the wife. She couldn't go to church, to a PTA meeting, or to her son's soccer game without people mentioning the post or just looking at her with pity. Even if they didn't say anything, she constantly felt like everyone was thinking about it. When her two children heard about the affair from their friends, the wife became so depressed and despondent that she refused to go out in public. One week later, feeling publicly shamed and humiliated, she filed for divorce.

From my perspective, adultery didn't kill this marriage.

Gossip did.

Before you post anything online, be absolutely certain you're not making something public that should be private. Do it to protect others. And do it to protect yourself. If you want close friends, you can't be perceived as a gossip. The Bible says, "When arguing with your neighbor, don't betray another person's secret. Others may *accuse you of gossip,* and you will *never regain your good reputation*" (Prov. 25:9–10 NLT, emphasis added).

Be trustworthy.

Keep what's private, private.

6.6 CONSUMING GOSSIP

The third set of questions you'll want to ask when gossip starts flying begins with this: "Am I permitting—maybe even encouraging—others to gossip?" It's not only wrong to dish it out; it's also wrong to eat it up. Scripture is clear: "*Wrongdoers eagerly listen to gossip;* liars pay close attention to slander" (Prov. 17:4 NLT, emphasis added). Notice that this verse doesn't say that only gossipers are wrongdoers. No, it says wrongdoers are also those who "*listen* to gossip." It's not just wrong to spread gossip; it's wrong to consume it. Why? Because what you permit, you promote.

Not only should you keep yourself from gossiping, you shouldn't associate with those who gossip. What is true "in person" is also true online. Because I am a Jesus follower, I do not develop close friendships with gossips; in the same way, I choose to avoid those who continually spray venom online.

For example, I used to follow a guy on Twitter whom I respect as a Christian author. He's written a couple of brilliant books that I've recommended to others and will continue to recommend. But I had to quit following him when I finally had enough. For whatever reason, his tweets became more negative than positive. Rather than showing love and promoting the things he was *for*, he kept correcting others and talking about things he was against. Twice in one week he said negative things about two pastors I know personally.

These last tweets bothered me so much that I picked up the phone and called him to ask if he knew these pastors and if he could prove what he had said. Not only did he *not* know these two pastors, he didn't have any evidence for his critical tweets. He told me he was simply repeating what he'd heard and offering his opinion. As a fellow Christian, I asked him not to spread rumors—especially when he didn't know the whole story. But when he continued tweeting in that negative, unsubstantiated way, I simply couldn't follow him anymore. If someone gossips *to* you, then they're likely to gossip *about* you. Stay clear of repeating gossip—and of hearing or seeing it.

> **If someone gossips *to* you, then they're likely to gossip *about* you.**

If someone is gossiping in person or online, you can be subtle in your approach to avoiding it. You can explain politely that you are not feeling comfortable with the conversation. If that's not your style, you can take a caring approach. Explain to the gossiper that if _____ (insert names) knew you were talking about them, you would hurt their feelings. (And if you're talking about them online, there's a pretty good chance they're going to know.)

Or you could help gossipers take an approach that is consistent with the teachings of Jesus. Remind them of Matthew 18:15–16, that if they have a problem with another brother or sister, they're supposed to do go directly to that person. And if all else fails to stop the gossipers, be direct and make the consequences clear. If they keep it up, you're not going to hang out with them anymore (or follow them, or whatever).

Any time I talk about someone else, whether in person or online, I want my words to be something I'd be willing to say in their presence. We should answer honestly, "Am I about to make private matters public?" When talking or posting, "Are my words helpful or hurtful?" Finally, "Am I permitting or encouraging others to gossip?" What we say (or allow others to say) matters because our words have the power of life and death (Prov. 18:21). I want my words always to be helpful, not hurtful. You know that old saying: you're either part of the problem or you're part of the solution. By God's grace, let's be a part of bringing solutions, not increasing problems.

6.7 YOU WILL GET SHOT

Even if you strive to answer these three sets of questions wisely and choose to be part of the solution online—and sometimes *particularly* because you've chosen to be part of the solution—you're still going to face others who are critical, harsh, or inappropriate toward you. If you choose to follow Jesus, you should never be surprised when you are persecuted. It comes with the territory.

For years, I knew that people were criticizing me and what our church was doing. But most of the time, I heard that criticism only from a distance. Then one day, it showed up on my doorstep. It was just a normal Saturday morning when my doorbell rang. When I answered, I saw a young guy, probably in his early twenties, grinning from ear to ear. I didn't recognize him, and he didn't seem to recognize me, so I was curious about why he was so happy. I didn't have long to wonder.

He launched into his story, telling me he had recently become a Christian. He was clearly thrilled to know Christ. Now he was going door to door, sharing his faith and inviting people to church. Before I could tell him I was a Christian too, he shifted into full-court-press witness mode, rapid fire, never taking a breath: "I was really bad and sinful, I mean I did lots of bad stuff, but then I called on God, well, Jesus, God's Son I mean, and he saved me and changed me and now I go to this amazing church and I want to invite you to go with me tomorrow so you can meet Jesus too—what do you say, will you go with me?"

I was delighted to see another person so passionate about his faith, and honestly, I wanted him to just keep talking. I was also curious to find out how effective this approach might be, whether he had been able to persuade other people to attend his church. But I also wanted to be polite, so I congratulated him on his new relationship, then told him I was already a Christian. Not only was he not deterred, but if anything, he was inspired. Taking a deep breath, he plunged in again, even faster than before, telling me why his was the best church in town and working to convince me that I should come see for myself. As he was talking, I realized that I knew his pastor. We had spoken several times, and he was always very nice.

I didn't want to say anything that might burst this kid's bubble, so I said simply, "Well, actually, I'm pretty involved already in the church where I go."

Beaming, he asked, "Really? What church is that?"

"LifeChurch."

His countenance collapsed. His face betrayed frustration, genuine concern, perhaps even a trace of pity. He leaned in close and began, much more slowly and deliberately than before, his tone just above a whisper, as though he didn't want anyone else to hear. "Listen . . . my pastor says," pausing to allow that spiritual authority to sink in, "that the pastor of LifeChurch . . . doesn't preach the truth."

He stood up straight, leaned back, and paused to achieve full effect. Then he started shaking his head slowly as he told me soberly, "You should never go back to that church. You don't want that false doctrine."

Honestly, these kinds of "revelations" didn't happen often back then. But with the blessings of today's technology, we can easily get as many as we want. If *anyone* says *anything* about us online, we can know instantly. We can even set up alerts to insure that we never miss a word of what's said about us. Unfortunately, because people can talk about us without having to face us—let alone actually identify themselves—then they're likely to do so more often than they would face to face. If we choose to stand up for our faith in Christ, I can guarantee that nonbelievers will take verbal shots at us. Unfortunately, as my front-door visitor demonstrated, we might even face friendly fire from within our own Christian family.

Jesus said something that may seem counterintuitive to us. "Blessed are those who are *persecuted because of righteousness,* for theirs is the kingdom of heaven. Blessed are you when people insult you, persecute you and falsely say all kinds of evil against you *because of me.* Rejoice and be glad, because great is your reward in heaven, for in the same way they persecuted the prophets who were before you" (Matt. 5:10–12, emphasis added). You don't have to do anything wrong to be persecuted. On the contrary, it's often what you do right that will draw criticism. But when people persecute you, you should consider it a blessing.

6.8 EXPECT, EMBRACE, ENDURE

That you should expect persecution probably isn't something you want to hear, but it is something you need to hear. Paul told his younger disciple Timothy, "In fact, *everyone* who wants to live a godly life in Christ Jesus *will be persecuted*" (2 Tim. 3:12, emphasis added). Did you see the first word I emphasized? *Everyone.* No matter who you are, how old you are, or how much you care about others, if you stand up for Jesus, someone will try to shoot you down. *Everyone* who wants to live a godly life will eventually be persecuted. Don't be shocked by this. Don't be discouraged by it. Don't be overwhelmed by it.

Expect it.

We've chosen to home educate our kids, and we're used to criticism about it. We know that some people disagree, so it doesn't bother us when they laugh or make fun of us. My favorite is when they say uninformed things like, "But your girls will grow up wearing denim skirts and churning their own butter." I usually respond with something like, "Well, they look lovely in denim skirts, and their butter is delicious." This criticism doesn't surprise us. We know it's coming.

Some of your friends may not like what you say on Facebook. They may talk behind your back. They may not invite you to some wild party they're having. Or you might even be overlooked for a promotion because you follow Jesus. None of these things surprise God. And they shouldn't surprise you. In fact, Jesus said, "If the world hates you, keep in mind that it hated me first. If you belonged to the world, it would love you as its own. As it is, you do not belong to the world, but I have chosen you out of the world. That is why the world hates you. Remember what I told you: 'A servant is not greater than his master.' *If they persecuted me, they will persecute you also*" (John 15:18–20, emphasis added). This is why I try never to worry when people shoot at me online for my faith. I actually worry when they don't.

> *Everyone* who wants to live a godly life will eventually be persecuted. Don't be shocked by this. Don't be discouraged by it. Don't be overwhelmed by it. Expect it.

Not only should you expect people to occasionally (or often) push back on your faith, but also when they do, you should endure it. Paul said, "When we are cursed, we bless; when we are persecuted, we *endure it*" (1 Cor. 4:12, emphasis added). Our example is Jesus on the cross. When the creation mocked the Creator, he didn't whine, gripe, or retaliate. Instead, he prayed for those who mocked and beat him. Jesus endured it. He rose above it.

When you're praying for others who are persecuting you, it's also wise to pray for yourself. If someone attacks, ask God to help you know how—or if—you should respond. Just because they shoot your way doesn't mean you have to answer. There are times you should answer and other times when you should ignore it. Either way, be careful not to react out of emotion; respond only in love.

While enduring persecution, you might reply with a thoughtful or encouraging comment. But remember that social media isn't a good place for long explanations. Just like a serious theological debate can't happen in 140 characters or less, it's hard to solve difficult problems in social media or email.

Don't feel pressured to respond. God can take care of himself; he doesn't need you to defend him every time some online heckler rattles your cage.

When critics flail at you, you aren't under any obligation to answer. Honestly, I can't remember the last time I responded to someone hurling bombs my way on social media. It's been at least five years now, maybe more. I often respond to people who have legitimate questions about our church, but I won't debate with people who simply want to pick a fight online. Pray and ask God if he wants you to respond.

I also encourage you to ask God to help you know when to listen and when to dismiss invalid criticism. If someone has a valid point and they're trying to help you, you should listen. Scripture confirms, "If you listen to *constructive criticism*, you will be *at home among the wise*. If you reject discipline, you only harm yourself. But if you listen to correction, you grow in understanding" (Prov. 15:31–32 NLT, emphasis added). But when strangers (or angry people) take cheap shots, you can often disregard what they're saying and move on. Don't let that poison seep into your heart.

Some people tend to be naturally critical and negative, but I choose not to let their foul disposition ruin a good day. It's also helpful to remember that sometimes people are simply hurting. Rather than taking their negative comments personally, I try to let them remind me to pray (in private) that they will experience God's healing. Peter describes how Jesus modeled this for us: "When they hurled their insults at him, he did not retaliate; when he suffered, he made no threats. Instead, he entrusted himself to him who judges justly" (1 Peter 2:23). In the middle of his pain, Jesus didn't fight back. Instead he allowed God to be his defender and submitted himself to the loving care of his heavenly Father. He calls us to do the same.

Someone once wrote a pretty negative article about our church and about me. Within minutes, the hateful comments started rolling in online. I regularly pray for thick skin and a soft heart, but I guess my skin was still way too thin and my heart nowhere near soft enough for these cruel people. By God's grace, I happened to be flying to another city later that day. Once our flight took off,

I didn't have access to what people were saying. (Remember back when planes didn't have Wi-Fi?) As our plane climbed higher and higher, rising toward the heavens, everything below looked smaller and smaller. For some reason, I felt closer to God above the clouds, and the problems on earth seemed small and distant. That's when it dawned on me: if I'm earthly-minded and self-centered, I will always feel the sting of critical people. But if I'm close to God and my life is his, then by faith—just like an ascending airplane—I can rise above the smaller-minded criticisms.

If you are facing persecution—or I should say *when* you face persecution—turn to God. Expect persecution. Endure it. By his power, even embrace it, as Peter advises. "Dear friends, *do not be surprised at the fiery ordeal that has come on you to test you,* as though something strange were happening to you. But rejoice inasmuch as you participate in the sufferings of Christ. . . . If you suffer as a Christian, do not be ashamed, *but praise God that you bear that name*" (1 Peter 4:12–13, 16, emphasis added). Don't be shocked when persecution comes. Take it another step: embrace it. Rejoice that in some small ways you are counted worthy to suffer with and for the one who suffered for you.

When someone says something cruel about you because of your faith, don't be ashamed. Instead, thank God that you belong to Jesus. Praise God that he's chosen you. Never react with some defensive or hateful rebuttal. As you're led and enabled by the Spirit, either respond in love or realize that you don't always have to respond. Ultimately God is your defender. And you live for him.

Yes, it's really tough when other people shoot at you. Believe me, I understand. All of us want to be liked by others. When you read a hundred positive comments about something you did and one negative one, which do you focus on most? If you're like me, it often takes only one negative voice to drown out all the positive ones.

Becoming obsessed with what people think about you is the quickest way to forget what God thinks about you. But the opposite is true as well. If you're living for Jesus in this selfie-centered world, you know a higher truth:

becoming obsessed with what God thinks about you is the quickest way to forget what people think about you.

By faith, stay out of the gossip. Rise above the criticism. When persecution comes, expect it. Endure it with the one who endured it for you. And by his power, embrace it, thanking God that he is with you.

And that's the truth.

Chapter 7

RECLAIMING WORSHIP

The Struggle with Idolatry

Idolatry is worshiping anything that ought to be used, or using anything that ought to be worshiped.

Augustine

I simply can't stop, no matter how hard I try. Once I post a picture, I go back immediately to see if someone liked it. Then because rarely does anyone click Like immediately, I'll refresh the screen again and again until someone does. Sometimes I'll even tell myself I'm going to wait ten minutes before checking again. But a minute or so later, I'm back for affirmation. And if a picture doesn't get at least twenty Likes in the first hour it's posted, I take the picture down. For some reason, I just can't leave one up unless it gets the response I want. I know I shouldn't be this obsessed with it, but I don't know how to stop.

Alyssa B.

It happened again—the third time this season. My son Aden is the star forward on his twelve-and-under traveling soccer team. While I was supposed to be watching the game, I somehow got sucked into looking at my phone. At first I was scanning a news app. Then I checked my Twitter feed. Then glanced at my stocks. That's when everyone started cheering. Aden had just scored, a rare and treasured left-footed goal. After missing his first goal because I was on my phone, I promised it would never happen again. But it happened in game two. And it just happened again. What's wrong with me?

Jerry M.

My husband told me I need to get control of it. And my body is telling me the same thing each morning when I can't drag myself out of bed. But for some reason, I can't control myself. Every night once the kids are in bed, I tell myself I'm just going to look on Pinterest for a few minutes. You know, just to unwind. But a few minutes turns into a few hours. Before I know it, it's 2:00 a.m. I'm embarrassed to admit it, but last night I was on until 3:30 a.m. I'm grumpy, exhausted, and so frustrated with myself. I promised myself I would go straight to bed tonight. But something tells me I won't.

Monica D.

7.1 SOUL SEDUCTION

There's a big difference between a baby's rattle and a baby rattlesnake.

Let me explain how I learned this the hard way. My second son is named Stephen, but in our family he's often called Bookie. (It started when Sam, Stephen's older brother, kept calling him Boobie—you can see the problem there. So we convinced Sam that Bookie was a much better alternative. We never expected it to stick.) When Bookie was only a toddler, I saw him jumping and squealing with joy on our front porch. "My fwend! My fwend!" he shouted exuberantly, twisting and turning with delight.

As I looked where he was pointing, I saw what appeared to be a baby toy, maybe a plastic rattle or an action figure left by one of the older kids, on the edge of the porch, just a few feet away. However when I got closer, I noticed his "fwend" started squirming and making noise—a baby rattlesnake! I almost knocked Bookie silly getting him out of the way so I could "take care" of his little fwend.

I will never forget that moment with my son, partially because it was both cute and dangerous at the same time. But it also offers a picture of how we often relate to something we think we need, something we love and can't seem to live without. Harmless enough at first, it eventually causes great harm in our lives. We're searching for something to meet our needs, only to be seduced by our dependence on a counterfeit that can hurt our souls.

Before you roll your eyes and think, "Here goes Craig again, off on another rant against technology, bless his heart," just hear me out. I truly love technology. I love social media. I love my apps. I love the games. I even love Siri (especially now that I have given her an Australian accent). I love reading books on my device. I love googling anything I want to know and getting immediate answers. And I love that GPS maps occasionally guide me to the right place.

But sometimes I wonder whether I love it all too much. Whether I adore it.

And I know I'm not the only one. Our reliance on technology seems to increase each day, each hour, each nanosecond.

No one would ever say, "Oh, yes, I do worship my iPhone—have you seen the new Burnt Offerings app?" Or, "I used to go to First Church of Facebook, but we were unfriended when we started attending virtual potlucks on Snapchat." When we think of idols, we often picture statues or figurines used by people of different religions or from ancient cultures. These idols can be natural objects, like rocks or trees, or something carved to represent the sacred object being worshiped.

If I asked you if you practice idolatry, you'd probably push back. "Don't be ridiculous! I don't worship statutes. Are you crazy?" I would do the same. But if you gain a better understanding of idolatry, your answer may change.

7.2 IDOL PLEASURES

God said, "So do not *corrupt yourselves* by making *an idol in any form*— whether of a man or a woman, an animal on the ground, a bird in the sky, a small animal that scurries along the ground, or a fish in the deepest sea. And when you look up into the sky and see the sun, moon, and stars—all the forces of heaven—don't be *seduced into worshiping them*" (Deut. 4:16–19 NLT, emphasis added). Here we see God dealing with a specific problem. On the edge of Canaanite land, his children faced the danger of temptation to worship golden calves, cedar poles, statues, and the moon and the sun that the Canaanites worshiped. Those things sound irrelevant and even silly to us because they seem to have no bearing on modern life.

Yet today, our pursuits and the things we give the majority of our time, money, and attention are no more worthy of worship. For instance, we are seduced by our social standing. How many followers do we have? How many

Likes did we get? Were we listed as a #mcm or #wcw? We ask, "Is the cute new person in school going to follow me?" Or, "Why hasn't that new account rep accepted my invitation on LinkedIn?"

Still resisting the possibility that you might be idolizing technology or what it provides? Think of it this way: someone said idolatry is making a good thing an ultimate thing. Idolatry is taking something—anything—and making it more important than it should be in our lives. Canadian preacher and theologian A. B. Simpson said, "As long as you want anything very much, especially more than you want God, it is an idol." Ouch. Timothy Keller defines idolatry this way in his book *Counterfeit Gods:* "An idol is whatever you look at and say, in your heart of hearts, 'If I have that, then I'll feel my life has meaning, then I'll know I have value, then I'll feel significant and secure.'"

Using these definitions and being honest, I have idols in my life. You might too. For years, most of us thought that what we need to be happy was some thing or someone. Maybe you thought the right car would change your life (or if you were like me at the age of seventeen, any car would've changed it). Or maybe for you it's a girlfriend or boyfriend, a husband or a wife. It could be a certain job or an impressive title, a corner office, or your own company expense account. It might be a certain amount of money in the bank or experiencing the perfect tropical vacation.

How have you filled in this blank for most of your life? If only I had _____, then I would be happy and fulfilled. Were you aware that this was replacing God in your life? How have you handled this idol?

Before social media, most of our idols were probably normal, predicable, visible, attainable, and pleasurable (at least temporarily). Now for the first time in history, we have a new category of potential idols to tame, ones that can be welcome distractions from our old, normal struggles with idolatry as well as idols in their own, life-proof shrine. Once again, we see how complicated #struggles can be.

These are idols that none of us predicted. We now have nonstop media feeding us micro-glimpses into the lives of almost everyone we know or admire. At the same time, we can see who thinks our lives are interesting enough to follow and receive immediate feedback on anything we feel is worthy of sharing. All of this is still new enough that we aren't totally sure how it's impacting us. But without question, it's hitting some more than others.

So let's consider how it's impacting us.

For example, we used to measure success by what we accomplished and what we accumulated. Because we didn't always know exactly what someone else had accumulated or accomplished, we had to guess where we ranked.

"I think I'm a little more successful than he is, but probably not her."

Now we have all the data before us. We can find out our CEO's salary, what kind of car our pastor drives, and what our kid's soccer coach paid for his new house. We can know how many followers our coworkers have and what our favorite celebrity wore grocery shopping last night. No longer do we have to guess or imagine who, where, when, why, and how. We have numbers, details, and real data. We can clearly measure Likes, shares, comments, retweets, etc. Instead of just estimating, we can have certainty.

"I know I have more followers than he does but only a fraction of the followers she has. And her pictures get three or four times the Likes that mine do. I know what he got paid last year, and his bonus was unbelievable. That's the twenty-third pair of new shoes she's posted this year, but who's counting?"

We tell ourselves over and over again that these kinds of measures of our worth don't really matter. They don't define us. They aren't who we really are. But we know that some people won't follow us if we don't have enough followers already. And Likes attract Likes, right? If people have no Likes, they won't likely get many more. But those with dozens seem to draw even more. We don't want to get our identity from what people think or who follows us, but it's increasingly tough not to do so.

7.3 VIRTUAL REALITY CHECK

A friend of mine who visited a remote, impoverished village in India told me a story. He saw a woman sacrificing a chicken as an act of worship to her god. My friend was shocked to see such blatant, modern-day idolatry. After striking up a conversation with the woman, he was impressed with her. She was well-spoken, kind, and educated.

When he learned that she had visited New York City three years earlier, he asked what she thought of America. She explained that she hated it. She had never seen more idolatry anywhere in her entire life. When my friend pressed her, she described three areas of idolatry that she saw.

First, she said, not so gently, that Americans worship their stomachs. Her eyes wide as she talked, this woman from a simple village described the massive stores overstocked with food to sell to people who had already had too much to eat. Evidently this woman was offended by people who are overweight when so many people in her village go hungry.

Second, she described how Americans worship television. From her perspective, they design their homes around the television. It takes the most prominent place in the most important room, and the furniture is arranged not for talking to people but for watching television. It was almost too much for her to comprehend that some people even allow a television in their bedroom—of all places!

Finally, she said the worst form of idolatry was in the relationship people have with their phones. She was deeply offended that people use them while driving. Even worse was that no one (at least in her experience) could have a full conversation without reading something on their phone.

Kind of gives a new meaning to American Idol, doesn't it? My friend didn't try to disagree with the Indian woman. He knew he couldn't. Everything she said was true. And she hadn't even scratched the surface.

Without getting into our obsessions with food and media, I'm simply raising the question about what we worship when we click. You are probably not putting a statue of a turtle ahead of God, and you probably aren't a star-worshiper, but is your obsession with your phone getting out of hand?

Some of us can honestly answer no. We are already using technology with good boundaries. We control it. It doesn't control us. We might have a healthy view of social media and how we interact with it. If so, I'm thankful, and you should be too!

Yet I know many well-intentioned followers of Jesus who are being se-duced, sucked into, and consumed by the virtual world. They think, "I just want to help my business." Or, "This will give more exposure to my ministry." Or, "I just love staying in touch with so many friends and family members."

My teenage daughters showed me the Instagram accounts of their friends and explained how some of them set up fake Likes. One teenage girl had only 112 followers. Her pics usually got thirty to forty Likes. But suddenly she would have four hundred or more Likes—with only 112 followers! Evidently she had an app that helped her obtain fake Likes. This makes absolutely no sense to me, but then, I'm not a sixth-grade girl. She certainly feels pressure that I don't know anything about. But I also know respected leaders who didn't have the number of Twitter followers they wanted, so they bought fake follow-ers to give the illusion of success. Seriously.

And I'm not above all this. About an hour ago, I tweeted. It had been awhile since I had said anything on Twitter, so I thought I should say something—you know, something short, memorable, catchy—of course connected to this book. So I typed, "At the end of your life, it won't matter how many LIKES you got but how much LOVE you showed." I added #struggles to it, just to make it complete.

Then I went back to writing this book, or at least trying to. Nearly an hour went by before curiosity got the best of me. I wondered how my less than 140 characters of spiritual brilliance had transformed the Twittersphere. So I checked to see how my tweet had performed in that first hour. Did people Like it? Favorite it? Comment about it? Retweet it? Drumroll, please . . .

The results: 134 favorites and 167 retweets.

If you have only eighty Twitter followers, you'd say that's out of the park. If you've got tens of thousands of followers, you might think that's about what you would expect. Not bad. Not great. If you are @mileycyrus, you'd think that was a slow minute. Something must be wrong with Twitter if that's all the action a tweet of hers got in a sixty-second period.

What's strange is that I'm not sure why I care whether anybody read my tweet. To this day, I've never heard anyone say that a tweet changed their life. I've tweeted some things that got a lot of attention while other tweets have been almost invisible, seemingly ignored and swallowed into the virtual grave for dead tweets. A few things I've said made a lot of people really mad. But nothing in my life or in the lives of those around me seems significantly different because of Twitter. My marriage has never been improved by a tweet. My kids aren't closer to God because of something I said on Twitter. Sure, someone might have been encouraged by a Bible verse. Or someone might have come to church who might not have otherwise. But overall, I can see no significant, measurable difference.

What if I had never sent a single tweet? What if Twitter didn't exist? Just a few years ago, it didn't. Humanity did fine for centuries without Twitter. When I look at it from that perspective, it really isn't that important.

Yet I felt compelled to check on my tweet. Curious. Had to know.

I'm still not quite sure why. I'd like to tell you that I don't really care about what my tweet did or didn't do. Part of me really thinks I don't care. But I still checked. I must #CareAtSomeLevel.

7.4 HOLY JEALOUSY

The last thing I want to do is make light of anyone's #struggles with social media. Peer pressure is crazy tough to deal with. But let's take an objective step back and ask ourselves, Are we being seduced? Are we placing too much value on something that's not that important? Are we bowing down and worshiping something besides God? Have we fallen into a new dimension of sin? Are our souls being seduced?

Jesus asked the question, "What good is it for someone to gain the whole world, yet forfeit their soul?" (Mark 8:36). We can adjust the question to today's culture: what good is it to get more followers, more Likes, more comments, more Pinterest pins, and yet forfeit our soul?

Is anything worth more than having a growing passion for our loving God? I don't think so.

And neither does God, who clearly doesn't pull any punches. With ultimate directness, he says, "You shall have no other gods before me. You shall not make for yourself an image in the form of anything in heaven above or on the earth beneath or in the waters below. You shall not bow down to them or worship them; for I, the LORD your God, am a jealous God" (Ex. 20:3–5).

That's pretty straightforward.

"You shall have no other gods before me."

God wants to be first in our lives. Second place is not acceptable. It's not sinful for God to be jealous in this way because for him, this is a holy jealousy, a righteous longing for our whole heart.

> Our news feeds can be full, but our hearts and souls empty. Anytime we allow our souls to be consumed with anything other than God, we will never be satisfied.

Why is it wrong to put other people or things before God? First, we need to realize that God is holy, eternal, omnipotent, and sovereign. He's . . . well . . . God, and we most definitely are not. Because he is God, he must be first. We need to understand that we are not a body with a soul. We are a soul with a body. Our bodies will die, but our souls will live forever. Our souls were created by God to be in intimate relationship with him. Our souls are created to know God, love him, worship him, and do life with him. That's why we must guard the affections of our soul and put him first.

Our souls can be seduced. We can be distracted. The pollution of this world can poison the purity of God's presence, making it harder to find him and be in relationship with him. That's why so many have to search so hard and why we try to meet our need for God with other things. But money, or things, or friends, or Likes, or followers, or whatever we think will make us happy never does make us happy. Our news feeds can be full, but our hearts and souls empty. Anytime we allow our souls to be consumed with anything other than God, we will never be satisfied.

Never.

7.5 KNOW THY SELFIE

You might not be obsessed with your phone (or with money or things or whatever). But if you're like most of us, you're coming dangerously close to idolizing yourself. Disguised and subverted in our reverence for technology is this sense that it empowers us to do anything we want to do. Yep, those commercials for the latest phone, app, tablet or laptop might as well promise superpowers.

As I mentioned earlier, approximately 80 percent of what people do on social media pertains to themselves. Just like that tweet I sent. I care about my tweet way more than anyone else does. (Jesus might have said to love other people's tweets as you love your own, but I don't think so. I'll keep working on that.)

Think about the whole notion of selfies for a minute, a phenomenon that still fascinates and repulses me in equal measure, like some kind of roadside accident on the information superhighway. I don't think the word *selfie* even existed a decade ago. Yet in 2013, the Oxford dictionary crowned it as their "word of the year." Seemingly out of nowhere, selfies have become an obsession for so many.

Pamela Rutledge said on *PsychologyToday.com*, "Selfies frequently trigger perceptions of self-indulgence or attention-seeking social dependence that raises the damned-if-you-do and damned-if-you-don't spectrum of either narcissism or very low self esteem."[17] It's not unusual for selfies to fill the vast majority of most teens' Instagram albums. This may be "normal," but it's certainly not healthy.

This story just makes me so unbelievably sad:

> Danny Bowman [a British teenager] says he became so obsessed with trying to capture just the "right" selfie that he ended up shooting about 200 pictures a day trying desperately to get a perfect representation of himself. And when Bowman failed to take what he perceived to be the perfect selfie, he attempted suicide with an overdose of drugs. Prior to his suicide attempt, Bowman says, he estimated he spent about ten hours every day taking selfies.[18]

When we contrast selfie-centeredness with what God requires—selfless surrender—the difference is striking. Jesus didn't say, "To be my disciple, you must promote yourself #SelfieSunday." He says the opposite. Jesus boldly proclaims, "Whoever wants to be my disciple must *deny themselves* and take up their cross and follow me" (Matt. 16:24, emphasis added).

Our culture says show yourself. Jesus says deny yourself.

If people look at your Facebook page, your Instagram pictures, or your most recent tweets, what will they see? Look over what you've posted, pinned, and tweeted in the past week or so

Our culture says show yourself. Jesus says deny yourself.

and be as objective as you can. Do you see a humble, others-focused, Christ-centered disciple? Or do you see someone other than who Christ has called you to be?

7.6 DETHRONING THE IDOLS

To learn more about how social media is impacting lives, I met with two dozen young adults who readily admitted they were addicted to their online world. Each person was also involved in serving in our church and was known for being close to God and making a difference in the lives of others. They all expressed excitement to talk about this subject, sharing a simultaneous love for what technology offers and yet a longing for something more. It struck me that every single person admitted two things:

1. They have an unhealthy addiction to social media or technology, but they have been unable or unwilling to admit it for some time.

2. They feel that they had lost passion for God because they are distracted by their passion for social media and technology.

It's important to look closely at these two confessions. First, all of these young adults know they have a problem. But for quite some time, they could not—or would not—admit it. I'm guessing you probably know someone like this. Chances are you can't have a whole conversation with some people without their checking email, glancing at Instagram, or posting something. That person may even be you.

Let's get real. If more than one person has told you that you have a problem, you probably do. Even if it's your mom or dad (who might have the same challenge as well), they may annoy you, but they still love you. If you can't get through a class, or a meeting, or a whole hour without looking, glancing, clicking, or stalking, you have a problem.

I don't want to sound harsh, and believe me, I have my own struggles, but if you're "buying" or acquiring fake Likes or followers, you need to stop for a moment and think about what you're doing. You're giving in to a pressure that feels very real, but what you're doing is wrong. It's not honest. It's not constructive. It's not healthy.

Maybe you are obsessed with fantasy football. You can't stop looking at your phone for updates and stressing over every catch, run, touchdown, and possible point. Now with NCAA fantasy football, you can spend your entire week making trades and talking smack about other players in the league. When football season is over, we have fantasy baseball and fantasy basketball to keep us going the rest of the year. A little fun is good. But you might have crossed the line, and I'm not talking about the goal line.

If you are checking multiple times a day to see what people are saying about you, let's call that what it is: idolatry. If your identity comes more from who follows you, who Likes you, what they say and what they think about you rather than who God says you are, it's time to take this issue to God.

Or you might be a person who compulsively checks email. Any time you see one come in, you just *have* to know what it says—immediately. Or maybe any time your phone buzzes, beeps, or dings, it draws you by some seemingly unstoppable force. If so, pause to consider: Are you drawn to the things of God in the same way? Or has the magnetic force of your phone become a stronger force in your life than the promised presence of God?

The second admission my young adult friends made is that they know their obsession is distracting them from God. Again, let me ask you to be honest. Do you think more about what God says in his Word or what people say on your feed? How much time do you think about God versus what to say online? Work hard to tell the truth. No matter how tempting it is to ignore him, if God is trying to get your attention, don't shake him off.

Have you made a good thing into a supreme thing, even above God?

David asked this question and then, inspired by God, he answered it: "Who may ascend the hill of the LORD? Who may stand in his holy place? He who has clean hands and a pure heart, who does not *lift up his soul to an idol*" (Ps. 24:3–4 NIV 1984, emphasis added). This imagery of lifting our souls to an idol strikes me. Are we trading our worship of the Trinity for something more along the lines of 4G LTE?

Is it possible that our soul, the part of us that no one sees but God, is secretly elevating our online presence above his eternal presence? Are we constantly pursuing something elusive? A black hole of empty promises? Are we believing that more of something other than God will fulfill us, satisfy us, and bring meaning to our lives? Is it possible that we've lifted our soul to an online idol? If we have, our soul still longs for more.

God is a jealous God. He wants to be first, above all else in our hearts and lives. So be honest about social media, or any other area of your life that you have put above God. It's time to tear the idols down.

7.7 JUST THE WAY YOU ARE

Years ago I was talking to a guy who was bragging about his wealth and detailing all the many ways God had blessed him. The guy had built a successful business that he was quite proud of. He described how much his profits had increased in the past five years and boasted about the value of his company. He told me about his second home in the ski resort of Aspen, Colorado, and the private jet he used for business trips and to shuttle his family back and forth on their frequent, exotic vacations.

Finally, I felt compelled to challenge him just a little bit. "You said that God blessed you. Do you feel any responsibility to use what God has given you to make a difference?" I fully expected him to soften, maybe even to backtrack and tell me about someone he had helped, perhaps describe some ministry or charity he supported financially. Maybe he hadn't wanted to brag about his giving or to reveal ways God had led him to invest in the kingdom. But the guy steamrolled ahead and calmly explained why he didn't feel compelled to give.

Dumbfounded, I asked him to clarify. "You mean you don't give *anything?* Like, nothing at all?"

Then he said something I'll never forget. Without reservation, he replied, "I don't give anything away because I love money. Love making it. Love spending it. Love what it buys. I love how it makes me feel. I earn my own money, so I use it on myself. Period." I imagine my jaw must have hit the floor, because then he added, "And don't go telling me how the love of money is the root of all evil. I've heard that before. That may be true for some people, but God and I are fine. He blesses me, and it's mine to spend the way I want. This is the way I am, and I'm not changing."

As shocked as I was, I appreciated his honesty and bluntness. My fear is that his attitude toward money is similar to how many people feel about technology. We might have a seriously dysfunctional relationship with our phones, our followers, or our Likes, but we don't care. We know something should change. But we just shrug it off. We might think, "I'm fine with it. I like it. This is just my thing. Even if it's wrong, even if God has something better for me, I don't care."

In the Old Testament, Gideon faced a similar problem with the people around him. They willingly bowed to idols and thumbed their noses at God in the process. But God was having none of it. With righteous passion, he told Gideon, "Tear down your father's altar to Baal and cut down the Asherah pole beside it" (Judg. 6:25). Notice that God didn't tell Gideon to help the people manage their idols, to shorten them by a few feet, just keep them under control. No, he commanded Gideon to tear them down. Cut down the poles. Don't tolerate the idols. Crush them. Destroy them. Smash them. Obliterate them.

If you know your unhealthy obsessions are interfering with your most important relationships—with people or with God—it's time to act.

Today.

This moment.

Now.

God doesn't want you to have *any* gods before him. Not a single one. God longs for you to know him, to enjoy his constant presence and goodness, to walk by his Spirit, and to live in his love.

When Jesus saw a rich guy who idolized his money and things, Scripture says, "Jesus looked at him *and loved him.* 'One thing you lack,' he said. 'Go, sell everything you have and give to the poor, and you will have treasure in heaven. Then come, follow me'" (Mark 10:21, emphasis added).

Don't miss Jesus' motivation here for asking so much of this rich guy. Jesus didn't tell the young man to give all his money to him and to his disciples, or to the building fund for the new temple. Jesus simply loved him. Do you see that? *Jesus loved him.* And Jesus loves you more than you can imagine. He doesn't want you to allow yourself to be seduced into settling for some counterfeit. He wants you to embrace his grace, satisfied in your soul, because he is not only all you need but more than you can imagine.

It's interesting to me that at least in the Gospel record, Jesus didn't tell anyone else to sell everything and give away all their money. This is the only time that Jesus gives such a specific command. Why did he tell this guy and no one else to get rid of everything? It's not because God doesn't want us to have money and things; it's that he doesn't want money and things to have us. Without question, the things of this world had this rich man's heart. They consumed him. He'd been seduced. And because Jesus loved him, he wanted him to have something better. So he commanded him to get rid of his idols and follow him.

If you sense the Spirit of God nudging you (or maybe it's more like a kick in the cursor), don't ignore him. He loves you. If your soul has been seduced into serving a counterfeit god, the one true God wants something better for you.

But gaining the better requires tearing down the idol.

Don't manage it.

Destroy it.

7.8 YEARNING AND TURNING

When I was in college, I was obsessed with popularity, parties, and girls. When I became a follower of Jesus, I managed to drop my need for popularity and skip the wild parties, but I was still pretty obsessed with finding a wife. If I couldn't be the campus playboy, then I figured I had better concentrate on the competitive world of Christian dating-leading-to-marriage. After a while, it became obvious this pursuit was an idol for me.

Realizing my behavior was out of balance, I decided to change my focus. For two years, I stopped dating altogether. Instead of pursuing a spouse with an intensity that would have put *The Bachelor* to shame, I sought God. I devoted most Saturday nights (my old party and date night) to praying, reading God's

Word, and seeking his heart. I had no idea at the time just how important this season would be for me. Little by little, my desire for what I wanted decreased, and my hunger for God's will became everything to me. It was only when he took the rightful place in my life that my heart was ready to love another person with his love. That idol came down, and my passion for God went up.

I don't know what tearing down your idols will mean for you, but if you can't get control, it might be time to do something drastic. I knew a girl (I'll call her Amber) who was so obsessed with her blog and online audience that her obsession was impacting her marriage, her friendships, her work performance, and her relationship with God. Many people tried to help Amber see that she was way past out of balance, but she resisted, fighting back and standing her ground.

Her husband finally got her attention when he said he was separating from her. In marriage counseling, she finally opened her eyes to the truth. She was idolizing her online image. Because Amber realized that she didn't have the ability to manage the problem, after a lot of prayer and counsel, she decided to eliminate it. She took down her blog, deleted her Twitter account, dismantled her Facebook page. Amber essentially stripped herself of everything that had been feeding her identity, so she could learn who she was as a child of God. With her spiritual relationship strengthening, she was then enabled to attempt to repair the other damaged relationships in her life.

I don't know how this story applies to you. Certainly not everyone needs to walk away from social media completely, but some might. If you recognize that you truly have an obsession, we'll talk more in the next chapter about some practical ways you can disconnect from good things and reconnect with the best things. You might also check out appendix 2 at the end of the book for some helpful ways to contain your tech usage. In the meantime, be sensitive to what God might be showing you. Is he leading you to make a change or try a different approach? What do you need to do to control your social media presence instead of letting it control you?

As you're cleansing your soul from idols, here's what will happen: you will begin finding room in your soul. If you used to check what people were saying on Twitter twenty times a day, but now you've cut back to just two times, you'll realize that you have more time to invest in something more meaningful.

So what should you do now?

I suggest that like never before, you decide to fill your soul with God. If your life has been full but your soul has felt empty, what do you have to lose? Give it a shot. Call on God. Pursue him with all you have and all you are. Seek him in prayer. As you taste and see that he is good, I'm convinced that you'll long for even more of his beauty. Psalm 107:9 says, "For [God] satisfies the longing soul, and the hungry soul he fills with good things" (ESV). If you feel empty, God's presence will fill and satisfy your soul.

I love when the psalmist says, "My soul yearns, even faints, for the courts of the LORD; my heart and my flesh cry out for the living God" (Ps. 84:2). This could be your prayer: "Instead of yearning for Likes, I'm yearning for your love, your presence, your goodness. My heart cries out to the living God." Or borrow the beautiful language from another psalm: "As the deer pants for streams of water, so my soul pants for you, my God. My soul thirsts for God, for the living God" (Ps. 42:1–2).

Do you relate to these words the psalmists used about God?

Longing?

Yearning?

Thirsting?

Panting?

If you're not experiencing these feelings for God, chances are your soul has been seduced by idols. It's time to destroy those idols and seek the God who satisfies your soul.

If you're not satisfied and are longing for something more, and you find yourself strangely drawn to your phone, your iPad, or your computer—as if they somehow hold satisfaction for your longing soul—then you need to reset your expectations of what they can deliver. Sure, they're tools that we can use and even enjoy. But you weren't made for Twitter. You weren't made to get

Likes on Instagram. You were made for God and to love him eternally. If you settle for anything less than living for him, then you've been seduced.

God has something better for you.

It's time to tear down the idols.

Long for God. Yearn for him. Thirst for his presence.

And let him satisfy your soul.

Chapter 8

REPLENISHING REST

The Struggle with Constant Distraction

Because God has made us for Himself, our hearts are restless until they rest in Him.

St. Augustine

When I have to sit still and focus on someone giving a presentation in a meeting, I get so fidgety. Even when I'm having a casual conversation with a friend over coffee, it's so hard not to just do a quick check to see if I have any new texts, emails, or updates. It's understandable if something important is going on, or my kids are sick. But my fingers get twitchy almost all the time if I'm not checking my phone every few minutes. I don't even realize I'm doing it sometimes! I hate it, but don't know how to break the habit.

Andrew L.

Last week I lost my phone, and I couldn't find it anywhere. For an entire day, I felt panicked and worried about what everyone who had contacted me would think, since I hadn't gotten back to them. That night I finally found my phone wedged under the floor mat in my car. No one had called me except the dentist's office to remind me of my upcoming appointment. My sister had texted me about a recipe for Mom's apple cake. And I had a dozen emails, nothing urgent or terribly important. But I felt so powerless and isolated without my phone. I hate feeling this way!

Patty S.

My boss is making me take a month-long sabbatical because she knows how burned out I feel. I'm way overdue for a vacation and have plenty of time, but I don't know what I'm supposed to do for a whole month that is going to be even close to relaxing. I'll be worried about what I'm missing and all the work that's piling up back at the office. I'm not even supposed to check my emails since my assistant will be responding to them all and calling me about anything truly urgent. Most people think of a sabbatical as a huge privilege, but I feel like I'm being punished.

Tom J.

8.1 BE VERY AFRAID

Do you suffer from *nomophobia?* Do you even know what it is?

According to *Psychology Today*, nomophobia is "the fear of being without a mobile device, or beyond mobile phone contact." Among today's high school and college students, it's on the rise. An increasing number of college students now *shower* with their cell phone.[19] One study showed that the average adolescent would rather lose a pinky-finger than their cell phone.[20]

Even if this information makes you laugh or roll your eyes, make no mistake: nomophobia is real. Studies have shown that about 66 percent of adults feel extreme anxiety if they lose connection with their mobile device.[21] You know, that feeling you have when your battery drops to 8 percent? Or that sick knot you feel in your stomach when you reach in your purse or pocket, and your phone's not where it usually is? More than half of the people who use a mobile device begin to feel upset when it's not with them.

Sound extreme? Well, guess what? If the age group is limited to eighteen to twenty-four, the percentage jumps to 77 percent.[22] Think about that number for just a moment. It means three in four young adults suffer anxiety when they're not connected through their technology.

The first time I read these numbers, honestly, I found them pretty difficult to believe. Then a few weeks later, our church hosted all of our staff members and their spouses for a three-day event. During one of the sessions, I handed my phone to my assistant so she could use it to complete a task for me. While I was talking with someone, she had to leave, and she took my phone with her. No big deal, right?

For about the first fifteen minutes of the next session, I didn't miss my phone. But then I thought of someone I needed to text, and when I reached for my phone, it wasn't there. Initially I panicked, but then I remembered my assistant still had it. After about thirty minutes without my phone, I became frustrated. Within forty-five minutes, I found myself slipping into full-blown anxiety mode. I was not amused by the irony that I couldn't text or call my assistant to ask where my phone was.

So I started looking around for someone else who might have her number on their phone, someone I could ask to contact her and explain what suddenly felt like an urgent problem. I felt so powerless and thought again and again, "Where could she be?" There was nothing I could do. But how was I supposed to run the world (or at least my world) without my phone?

Then it hit me: maybe those percentages weren't so far off after all.

According to one study, 58 percent of people say they won't go one waking hour without checking their phone; 59 percent check their email as soon as it comes in; and 89 percent check their email every single day they're on vacation. Another study says that 87 percent of teenagers sleep with their phones.[23] I'm sorry, but if you're sleeping with your phone, you need help. You need counseling. You need Jesus. And someone needs to take your phone away from you for eight hours while you sleep.

Eighty-four percent of people said they couldn't go one day without their phones.[24] That's the power of nomophobia in action. It's incredibly real. And it's increasingly common.

8.2 CYBER SABBATH

Let me ask you a few questions, and I want you to answer as honestly as you can. You should never lie to anyone, but remember, I'm a pastor, so it's even worse if you lie to me. (I'd hate for lightning to strike you where you're sitting and leave just the charred remains of your phone case.)

Is checking your phone the last thing you do every day?

What about when you wake up? Is checking your phone one of the first things you do every morning?

Do you feel compelled to check your phone while waiting in line at the fast food drive through, in the checkout lane at the store, or while waiting in the airport? More than once?

Would you rather give a mugger your purse or wallet than your phone?

If you answered yes to any of these questions, maybe it's time to power down and take a cyber Sabbath. Maybe it's time to remember what life is like without your phone, tablet, or laptop. Maybe it's time for your soul to rest.

You might think that because I'm a pastor, I don't have these #struggles. But believe me: I do, just as much as anyone else. While thinking about this topic, I knew I had to look at my own habits. At the end of the day that I discovered the meaning of nomophobia, I received three texts after 10:45 p.m. Around 11:15, as I was about to go to bed, I checked my email one last time and discovered several messages I hadn't read yet. One in particular really upset me, and to make matters worse, I could do nothing about it right then. So I just lay there in bed, alternating between trying to sleep and staring at the ceiling in the dark, stewing. I had not mastered technology that night; it had mastered me.

I suspect I'm not the only one. I believe that a lot of us have a hard time tuning out and shutting down. Many of us, when we're bored, when we don't have anything else going on, or when we're between tasks or conversations have a default, brain-off habit of picking up our mobile devices and lazily clicking around.

Many of us, when we're bored, have a default, brain-off habit of picking up our mobile devices and lazily clicking around.

When our minds are idle, we're not thinking about anything meaningful, and when we're not intentionally living, it can be so easy to shift into neutral. When we don't have a specific destination in mind, any road will do. And if our time and our resources aren't precious, if we're not doing anything important, it can be so easy to just pick up our phone, unlock the screen, and wander aimlessly through cyberspace, wasting our time and our thoughts.

Because we constantly allow ourselves to be distracted, because we don't take our thoughts captive in obedience to Christ, our minds never shut down. So we're constantly distracted. We can't work productively for long stretches because we allow something to ping or beep and break our concentration. We let our RPMs run all the time, constantly revving our mental and emotional engines. We feel overwhelmed, and we don't know why. We're short with our children, and we don't know why. We feel exhausted spiritually, and we don't know why. We long for something more. Ironically, we keep returning to the source of our discontent, and of course we won't find peace there.

Something has to change.

8.3 JESUS CALLING

Most people in our culture accept the fact that our bodies need rest. However, I'd argue that our souls need rest just as much. Our souls need to be disconnected *bing!* long enough to find peace *bing!* and some solitude in the presence of the God *bing!* who created us to know him, *bing!* to walk daily with him, *bing!* to be in an intimate, ongoing, thriving relationship with him, *bing!* representing his love in this world *bing!* rather than being wrapped up all the time *bing!* with some little device that absolutely demands our attention.

Can you feel what I'm saying?

Speaking to the church at Corinth, the apostle Paul says, "'I have the right to do anything,' you say—but not everything is beneficial. 'I have the right to do anything'—but I will not be mastered by anything" (1 Cor. 6:12). When Paul wrote this letter to the Corinthians, he was responding to all sorts of perverted and sinful actions that he had learned they were doing. He was trying to express to them that in Christ, we have freedom to do many things. However—and you probably don't need me to tell you this—just because we *can* do a thing doesn't mean that we *should* do it.

What Paul says here is one of my favorite verses in Scripture: "'I have the right to do anything,' but I will not be mastered by anything." The power of Christ in me should be stronger than anything else in my life. I will not be mastered by an addiction to food. I will not be mastered by material possessions. I will not be mastered by an addiction to looking at things that are inappropriate for me to see. I will not be mastered by what other people think of me.

I will not be mastered by technology.

But sometimes I am.

I love technology, but I have to stay mindful to refuse to be mastered by it. Christ in me is stronger than any addiction in me.

Christ in you is stronger than any addiction in you. We will not be mastered.

Christ in you is stronger than any addiction in you. We will not be mastered.

If you're constantly connected, and you find yourself feeling that low-grade frustration—"There has to be something more, there has to be something more, there has to be something more"—then I'm going to argue that God has a special rest for you in Christ. You need to know that his rest is available to your soul.

And it's available right now: "So there is a special rest still waiting for the people of God. For all who have entered into God's rest have rested from their labors, just as God did after creating the world. So let us do our best to enter that rest. But if we disobey God, as the people of Israel did, we will fall" (Heb. 4:9–11 NLT).

Why is it so hard for us to find this rest? And what is that one thing we're actually longing for? I quoted St. Augustine at the beginning of this chapter, and I hope his words resonate with you. God made us to be in relationship with him. So our hearts are restless until they rest in him.

This explains why our souls have been restless for so long, why we keep looking online for something that can satisfy our longing. Our souls need something that can bring meaning, something that can help our relationships work, something that can give us purpose and significance, something that fills the void inside of us once and for all. This is the central issue: we have a Jesus-shaped void inside of us. And nothing besides Jesus is ever going to fill that vacancy.

Jesus longs to give us what we so desperately crave: "Come to me, all you who are weary and burdened, and I will give you rest. Take my yoke upon you and learn from me, for I am gentle and humble in heart, and you will find rest for your souls" (Matt. 11:28–29).

Are you weary? Do you feel burdened? Come to Jesus. His invitation is for you. Come to him now. Come to him by faith, and he'll give you rest. He's gentle. His heart is humble. Jesus is offering you his special rest.

But in order to fully experience his rest, you're going to have to focus your heart on him and him alone. Nothing else. No one else.

Only Jesus.

8.4 ALL IS CALM

This is where the rubber meets the road. What are you going to choose? Are you going to do whatever it is that you feel God leading you to do? Or are you just going to try to numb that still, small voice and go on with your life as it has been? Really, it's up to you. But maybe you're wondering, "How? How do I come to him? That sounds great, but how do I find rest in God?"

You can start doing two things right now. The first is simple: learn to be still. Look at what the psalmist says about God:

> He says, "Be still, and know that I am God;
> I will be exalted among the nations,
> I will be exalted in the earth."
>
> —*Psalm 46:10*

Learn to be disconnected and still in the presence of God.

Be still.

Focus.

Focus on God.

Have you ever been around a little kid who just can't seem to sit still? Maybe you have a kid like that. (You may even be married to a big kid like that.) Sometimes you just want to tell them, "Sit still or else!"

In one of his psalms, David declares, "I have calmed and quieted myself" (Ps. 131:2). Notice he indicates that it's possible to *choose* to do this. David's soul wasn't just calmed somehow, by accident. He calmed it himself. He did it on purpose. He didn't wake up one morning, start checking his phone, and say, "Oh, looks like I've got some new emails, a couple of texts, and some notifications. Say, that reminds me: I sure do feel still!" No, David chose to calm himself. He quieted himself. He decided to be still.

We can learn to do the same thing. It's not easy. It definitely requires practice. Sometimes we just have to tell our souls to chill. "Cool it, soul. Don't get so wound up. Sit down. Rest. Take a breather." David chose to switch gears mentally and focus on finding a state of calm and quiet.

How do I know you can do this? Because I learned the hard way. And if I can learn how to still myself before God, anyone can.

8.5 JUST FIVE MINUTES

Two different times in my life I have gone to counseling to address workaholic issues. The first time I went to see a counselor to discuss this problem, my boss told me I had to. Back then I was young and secretly thumbed my nose at his concern for how driven I was. I thought, "Why would anyone have to get counseling for that? Man, you say workaholic; I say disciplined. We should all be getting more things done every day! If being super focused and productive is a crime, then guilty as charged."

But the second time . . . well, that was different. I had come to the painful conclusion that I was trapped in a nonstop nightmare of my own making. It didn't matter how hard I worked or how long I worked; I was never caught up. There was always so much left to do. I woke up every morning already feeling behind, which only made me work faster, stay longer, and try harder. But I couldn't keep it up. I was exhausted and frustrated, and I knew something had to change. I couldn't live like this. I knew work had become an idol, one

I justified because I was "working for God." But I also knew he wanted me to rest, and I couldn't.

So I saw a counselor because I needed help if anything was going to change. I had tried to fight this problem by myself, tried to figure it out, but work was mastering me. The grind was destroying my body, my mind, and my life.

The counselor heard me out and asked several questions. Eventually, he helped me see the pattern I was trapped in. He said, "Your body is addicted to adrenaline. That little shot you feel every time you complete something? That's a drug being released in your brain. Just like heroin or some other narcotic, your body craves that spike, and it's forever chasing it."

I realized that what he was saying was absolutely true, so of course I was willing to do anything I could to overcome it. But to me, his solution sounded like the dumbest thing anyone had ever said. "You need to learn how to shut down. You need to schedule five minutes a day, every day, when you just do nothing. That's it. Don't do anything. Don't think anything. Just be still before God. Put it on your calendar, and then stick to it."

I listened to him respectfully, but I was thinking, "You don't know what you're talking about. Do you have any idea how much I still have left to do? I don't have time to do nothing! I'm paying you ninety-five dollars an hour for this advice, and this is what you're giving me?"

I couldn't see it at the time, but looking back on it now, I realize that even the very idea was stressing me. Do nothing? For five minutes? How ridiculous and stupid! Anybody can do nothing for five minutes—easy!

And then I tried it. It was one of the hardest things I've ever tried to do in my entire life. Picture this: your five-minute "do nothing" time pops up on your calendar. So you set a timer for five minutes, set your phone face down on the desk, fold your hands, close your eyes, and try to clear your mind.

Bing!

My mind instantly started reeling. "Wait! What was that? What just happened? What am I missing? Was that an important email? Is that a text I need to respond to? What if Amy needs me? What if one of our kids is hurt? Did somebody just post a picture of their coffee with a swirly on top? Did somebody just Like the picture I posted of my lunch? What's happening? What's going on out there? What am I missing?"

Laugh all you want, but I dare you to try it.

Five minutes, completely still.

At first it feels impossible because your mind starts unloading all the items you've been too distracted to notice.

"I need to get that stuff done in the yard."

"Shh," God says. "Relax."

"What am I going to make for dinner tonight?"

God says, "Be still."

"Do I need to get milk on the way home?"

God says, "Quiet your soul."

"If the baby's diaper doesn't get changed, it's gonna be a mess."

God says, "I am God."

"I heard somebody say they were going to reschedule that meeting tomorrow. Have I gotten the new time and the room number?"

God says, "Can you hear me?"

"I don't have time to just sit here right now! I'll forget all these things that need to be done!"

"Be still," God says, "and know that I am God."

Just five minutes. Can you do it? Or is something mastering you? Do you constantly have to check what's going on

> Is something mastering you? Do you constantly have to check what's going on in other people's lives? Or can you find the discipline, by the power that raised Christ from the dead and now lives in you, to just be still?

in other people's lives? Or can you find the discipline, by the power that raised Christ from the dead and now lives inside of you, to just . . . be . . . still?

Can you do it?

Can you be still?

Can you contemplate the goodness of God?

Can you just know that he is God?

Take a deep breath.

8.6 CAN YOU HEAR ME?

Getting quiet is just the first part. I'd argue that the second thing you need to do is more important, but you can't do it until you've gotten quiet. After you've found a way to silence the noise and you reach a quiet place and have calmed your soul, then simply listen.

Listen.

Can you hear him?

Listen for God's still, small voice.

Like getting quiet, of course, listening doesn't happen by accident. You need a plan to do it, because you will never find a break in the action of distraction when you can hear God talking to you through all the noise. You have to be deliberate and make a plan. The Bible describes such preparation as part of being wise: "A wise man thinks ahead; a fool doesn't and even brags about it!" (Prov. 13:16 LB).

It couldn't be clearer that it's foolish *not* to make a plan. Yet we all know people like this. They say things like, "It's no big deal. I just like to see where the day takes me. It'll work out somehow." The problem is when we try to "go with the flow," we end up having to stomp out little fires all day, every day, as they spring up. We live our lives in reaction mode. Every new issue that crops up has the potential to be an emergency or a crisis. Our priorities suffer because we let distractions consume us. So we have to plan ahead for how and when we're going to get quiet so we can hear God.

If you think listening to God is no big deal, then I have to tell you, as respectfully as I can, such thoughts are foolish. If you neglect your time with God because you keep allowing yourself to be distracted, you're missing out on an intimate connection with him. Your relationship with God is similar to other relationships in your life. If you neglect the important people in your life because you keep interrupting your time together, then you're hurting them. If you're checking your fantasy football results while trying to have a conversation with your wife, she will feel slighted. If you're checking Facebook or blogging instead of helping your kids with homework, then they'll assume they're not important enough to merit your time. If you can't unplug for at least a few minutes each day to be still and listen to what God may want to say to you, then you are sending him the same kind of message.

> If you neglect your time with God because you keep allowing yourself to be distracted, you're missing out on an intimate connection with him.

I'll never forget when Amy told me straight up, "You shouldn't let your phone interrupt our family time together at dinner. The church can survive forty-five minutes without you." She could not have been more right. It was uncomfortable, but it was something I needed to hear. But I had to make a plan to change my bad habit.

A good plan has two parts: a defense and an offense. Our defense is the strategies we put in place to protect ourselves from the influences we know are going to try to sweep us off the playing field. But we will not be mastered by anything. The power of Christ within us is greater than any addiction we have and stronger than the gravity of anything that's trying to pull us away from him. We're not going to let anything separate us from the love of God that we have in Christ (Rom. 8:35–39). Our offense is the direction we point our lives in, the actions that we take to travel where we believe God wants us to go.

8.7 DO NOT DISTURB

If you want to experience real soul rest, make a plan that includes both your defense and your offense. Each plan is personal, so I don't know what yours will look like for you. But you have to make it. Maybe your defense should begin with asking the people in your life—your spouse, your children, your family, your friends, the people around you who care about you—to help you lay down some ground rules.

Maybe when you're together for a meal, all the phones will be silenced and vibration turned off, and they will be placed face down in the middle of the table. I have some friends who have a basket by their refrigerator for this purpose. When everyone comes to dinner, they turn off their phones and put them in the basket. Nobody gets their phone until dinner is over and Mom and Dad pass them back out. This is a pretty easy place to start. You don't have to keep this defense just within your family, either. Maybe you should use the same defense during your small group or time with the friends you're doing life with.

Amy and I put a defense in place when I was studying the material for this book. We have all of our kids ready for bed at 9:00 p.m. The older kids have a later bedtime than that, but everybody is ready and tucked in by then. At 10:00 p.m., we put our phones in "do not disturb" mode and plug them into their chargers for the night. Between 10:00 p.m. and 7:00 a.m. is our time. We're out. (In a legitimate emergency, of course, our kids have other ways to reach us. They can come knock on our bedroom door, for example.)

While this defense works for us, you will need to figure out what's appropriate for your situation. Don't let yourself be mastered by anything. Lock it down and push it away from you, as far away as you have to, until you master it.

Maybe your defense is to turn off all of your social media notifications. Lock that *bing!* out of your life. Be honest with yourself: you don't really need to know the instant somebody's cat gets the sniffles. Does seeing the antelope a barista drew in the foam on your cousin's coffee draw you closer to God? It can wait! I'm not saying you shouldn't look at social media at all. Just schedule the time when you do it. Master it; don't let it master you. You determine when you connect and check and when you turn it off.

Sometimes when I really need to focus on something—like, say, a message for the upcoming weekend at church—I may leave my phone with my assistant with instructions not to interrupt me unless Amy or one of my kids needs me. I can trust my assistant to handle anything else that comes up, or it can wait. But sometimes I need six hours in God's Word to pull a message together, and I'm not going to let some silly distraction take me away from something so important. This is just one example that applies to me. But you can use it to figure out what you can do that will work in your circumstances.

Maybe you need to plan periodic breaks from social media and put them on your calendar. If you're going on vacation, you might choose not to check your social media. Then every day you're on vacation, you focus all of your attention on the people you're with, the people you love who love you, instead of looking at what other people are doing. Maybe just a few days isn't long enough for you. Maybe what you need is a month-long break. Why? Because you're totally mastered by social media. If you find that you can't go a month without it, you will really learn something about where your true priorities are. My purpose is not to tell you what to do. I just want to get you thinking about your own defensive plan.

8.8 REST FOR YOUR SOUL

Finally, in addition to good defensive measures, you need to develop an offensive plan. I like to take advantage of the primary tool I use to relate to God. Instead of just allowing social media to be the default thing I checked each morning and looking to see what everybody else is up to, I asked myself, "What would be the highest, best use of my phone?" And it dawned on me that the best thing I could do first thing in the morning is open up that day's reading from a Bible plan in the YouVersion Bible App. Although honestly, it may be the second thing, because I usually have to go to the bathroom first. (I'm sure God understands.)

Maybe something like that would be a good thing for you to put into your offensive plan—the Bible part, I mean. What's your plan to get yourself into God's Word and really connect with it? Engage with it? Feed on it? Let it build your soul, renew your mind, and transform you into the image of Christ?

Like my counselor advised me, maybe you need to commit to five minutes of solitude a day, a sacred time to simply contemplate the goodness of God. Maybe you need something more involved, to establish a consistent, focused prayer time when you commit to letting God's presence pour over you during a focused prayer time. Maybe you need to seek God about some things and then carry them with you throughout your day, praying over them for a few seconds each time they come up in your memory.

Maybe you need to practice having a constant spirit of worship, not just coming to church and singing a few songs on the weekend, but learning some worship songs and either playing them throughout your day or singing them in your mind all the time. Maybe directing your heart toward God like this is a good way for you to connect with him, gradually adding different forms of worship the longer you do it. Let worship grow into something that is not just what you do but part of who you are and a strategic part of your offensive plan to grow closer to God.

Maybe it's time for you to reconsider the world around you—actually go outdoors, look around, and recognize and acknowledge the awesome creative power of God. Consider the wonder, the glory, the extravagance of all that he's created, both for his worship and our pleasure. The world he has given us to live in demonstrates that the rocks will cry out to him in worship, even if we won't (Luke 19:40). Watch a sunset. Bask in God's power in creating it, the genius of its color and light. Just let your soul soak up its beauty.

> Watch a sunset. Bask in God's power in creating it, the genius of its color and light. Just let your soul soak up its beauty. Resist the temptation to take a picture of it.

Resist the temptation to take a picture of it. But if you just can't help it, keep the picture as something that's between you and God. Don't post the photo online; you don't need Likes for something God created for you to love. Cherish the moment with him in his presence and thank him for it rather than corrupting it by using it to feed your ego.

Figure out your defensive and offensive plans. Talk with the people you do life with to come up with realistic solutions that will help you master once and for all the things that have been mastering you. Get serious about this. You may even learn that people who love you have already been praying for you to overcome these things. Don't allow yourself to be mastered by anything!

Finally, it all comes down to this:

> This is what the LORD says:
> "Stand at the crossroads and look;
>   ask for the ancient paths,
> ask where the good way is, and walk in it,
>   and you will find rest for your souls."
>   —*Jeremiah 6:16*

Are you standing at a crossroad? What decision do you need to make? Identify it. Call it by name. Which way should you take? What ancient paths can inform your choice? Sometimes ancient spiritual disciplines, tried and true, are better than new technologies. They include fasting, prayer, solitude, and seeking the goodness of God.

Ask him, "Father, where is the good way? What do you want me to do? What choice should I make that will bring honor to you?"

Once you are quiet and listening, and you feel God has told you the good way, *start walking in it*. Don't put it off. Don't make excuses. When you walk in God's good ways, you'll find the rest your soul is crying out for. Be still and know that there is only one who truly loves you, and only he is more deserving of your worship than anything you'll ever find on this earth. Put him first. Seek him with all of your heart, and he will add everything that matters.

Be still and know that he is God.

Conclusion

KEEPING TECHNOLOGY IN ITS PLACE

My favorite things in life don't cost any money. It's really clear that the most precious resource we all have is time.

Steve Jobs

Every year for the last dozen years or so, our friends the Liddells have invited us to spend a weekend with them at their lake house. It's hard to describe how much we enjoy and look forward to this annual weekend getaway. We love it for several reasons. The Liddells are close friends, and any time with them is always a good time. Diane Liddell always goes a little crazy on the food. No one ever goes hungry, and we eat like the calories don't count. And of course going out on the water, pulling kids on tubes, and riding jet skis is a total blast.

But it finally dawned on me that there's another reason I love going to the lake so much: our phones don't work there. Lost in the back roads of rural Oklahoma, we're out of reach of the cell towers. The first time we went and couldn't use our phones, I climbed the walls. But once I realized I could do nothing about it, I accepted our "cell-free zone" as a blessing and not a curse. While I still had to fight the impulse to keep checking my phone every five minutes like I normally would, it felt good to know I was completely "off duty" to the rest of the world.

It's gotten easier every time we go. Now, since we know we'll be hard to reach, we tell a few people—my parents, Amy's parents, my assistant, and a couple of other friends—that we'll be away from our phones for most of the weekend. Knowing our phones can't reach social media, that we can't surf the web, and that texts won't come through, we just put the phones aside on Friday night and don't touch them again until we start toward home on Sunday evening. Crazy, right?

The last time we went to the lake, I couldn't wait to turn my phone off. Then it dawned on me. I'm available every day of the year, tied to a device except for one weekend when I'm beyond the grasp of technology. And that weekend has consistently been my favorite time of the year.

As I've confessed, I know something has to change in my relationship with technology. While I'd never dream of walking away from all the life-enhancing benefits (nor would I ask anyone else to), I refuse to be enslaved by something that's supposed to be a convenience, an enhancement, a blessing.

So I'm making some changes.

After reading this book, I hope you will want to make some changes too. If you're tired of the way technology enslaves you rather than serves you, then allow Jesus to do a healing work in you to enable you to move forward by his grace and for his glory. You'll realize that healing is always available and is an ongoing process. God was around long before you took your first selfie or posted your #WorldsBestBurger recipe online, and he'll be around a long time after.

He's more powerful than any idol and more loving than any friend on Facebook or follower on Instagram. He's more than willing to help you change if you just let him.

DO YOU WANT TO GET WELL?

So if you want to change the way you relate to technology and social media, then I encourage you to consider the story of someone who asked Jesus for help when he needed to be healed. In John 5:1–15, we're told how one day Jesus approached the pool of Bethesda in Jerusalem, a place where sick people gathered. There were people who were blind, likely lame people, and possibly someone who was paralyzed.

These people gathered and waited patiently because they believed an angel would stir up the water causing bubbles to rise. Like people for centuries before and since and in other places, the people of Jerusalem believed the bubbly waters had healing powers, and needy people embraced the legend that the first person in the water would be healed.

One guy stood out as Jesus approached the crowd of hurting people, a man who had been an invalid for thirty-eight years. *Thirty-eight years.* We can only imagine how hard this guy's life was. For thirty-eight years, he couldn't work. For thirty-eight years, he couldn't walk. For thirty-eight years, he was dependent on other people to do everything we do ourselves and take for granted. Thirty-eight *days* of suffering is difficult to endure. Thirty-eight *years* must have seemed like an eternity.

This reality makes Jesus' question to this man stand out even more. "When Jesus saw him lying there and learned that he had been in this condition for a long time, he asked him, '*Do you want to get well?*'" (John 5:6, emphasis added). What kind of question is that to ask to a guy who's been unable to walk for almost four decades? This question seems insensitive, almost insulting. It's like asking a broke guy if he wants to win the lottery. It's like asking a hungry guy if he wants a year's worth of free food at his favorite restaurant. It's like Amy asking me if I want to make out. (Sorry about that last one. I just got on a roll.) Why would Jesus ask such an obvious question?

Because Jesus needed to know if the guy really wanted to change.

Because Jesus knew this guy needed to know for himself if he really wanted to change.

Did he *really* want to be well?

You might have picked up this book because you're a bit like me. You have a love-hate relationship with technology. You love it for all the obvious reasons. But you hate that it consumes you and that your default action in any slow moment of life is to start going *click, swipe, swipe, swipe, click.*

Maybe you've had a problem with technology for a while. It's distracting you from those in front of you. People you care about often complain because you're staring at your phone and not listening to them. You can't go an hour without checking your device. If you don't have it with you at all times, you feel lost, vulnerable, and anxious. Maybe your identity is wrapped up in Likes, comments, and retweets. If you gain a follower, you're happy. But if you lose one, you get upset. You know you shouldn't be like this, but you are. And when you're honest, it bothers you.

If you've been chained to this addiction for a while, you might recognize three major challenges that make it harder to break free.

1. The longer a problem persists, the more discouraged you become. For thirty-eight years, nothing changed for the poor guy at the pool of Bethesda. Similarly for who knows how long, your device may have been keeping you from being fully alive in Christ. Maybe you've tried to manage it, but you just can't. So you're tempted to resign yourself to it, saying, "Hey, everyone else is tied to theirs, right? So this is just the way life is going to be. I wish I could change, but we all know that will never happen."

2. The longer a problem persists, the more excuses you make. When Jesus asked the man if he wanted to be well, the man replied, "Sir, I have no one to help me into the pool when the water is stirred" (John 5:7). He explained to Jesus that because he had no help, everyone else raced by him, leaving him stranded without any hope. Maybe this describes where you are today. You want to change, and you secretly hope that somehow God will help you. But you also know it's easier to just wait by the pool and make excuses than to crawl over and dive in. You may be saying something like this:

- "I can't live without my phone for an hour, much less a whole day."
- "It's just the way life is today. Staying current is too important to me."
- "Besides, I tried to unplug once, but it just wasn't worth it."

3. The longer a problem persists, the more you learn to compensate. Just like the functional alcoholic who manages to perform well on the job while being a wrecking ball at home, you may be able to get around your techno-dysfunction. You keep passing your classes. You keep getting your job done. And by all means, you keep current on what's happening in other people's lives and still manage to make time for the perfect #SelfieSunday pic.

But your life is full of things that aren't satisfying you.

You know there has to be more.

You long for it, but you don't know where to find it.

So here's the bottom line: you cannot change what you are willing to tolerate. If you just sort of don't like it, the problem won't go away. Not ever.

If you're willing to put up with it, things will never be different. You have to get to the point where you're no longer afraid of what you might miss out on. You have to refuse to miss out on what—and who—is right in front of you.

FAITHFUL OR FAMILIAR?

Maybe you can sense the Spirit of God posing Jesus' question to you.

Do you want to be well? Do you really? Do you want to enjoy the blessings of technology without being a slave to it? Are you willing to do whatever it takes to put God first in your life?

If you are, then something must change.

Someone once asked me, "Craig, what do you think is the greatest hindrance to faith?" Lots of possibilities ran through my mind. Worry is certainly a hindrance to faith, right? So is doubt. You could also argue that fear really undermines faith. And God has not given us a spirit of fear (2 Tim. 1:7 NLT). But as I pondered all these contenders, another one came to mind that is less obvious, but just as dangerous.

> Do you want to be well? Do you want to enjoy the blessings of technology without being a slave to it? Are you willing to do whatever it takes to put God first in your life? If you are, then something must change.

Perhaps *the familiar* is the greatest enemy to faith.

Instead of believing that God can do anything, many surrender to what they see. They accept what is instead of what could be. Maybe you've become comfortable with your addiction to technology. You've learned to rationalize it, to explain it away. You tell yourself it's really not that big of a deal. Maybe everyone you know is a lot like you, so it couldn't really be that bad, could it?

Perhaps the familiar, what you know and accept, is the greatest obstacle to your faith. Faith in what could be. Faith in what God calls you to be.

The invalid could have argued, "I've never been able to walk. I've always been dependent on others. No one will ever help me." You might have your excuses: "I've got to be on my phone 24/7. If I'm not, how will they reach me? I have to stay in touch with what's going on. I can't do my job without my phone."

If the familiar is the greatest obstacle to faith, then it takes faith to step away from the familiar.

Maybe that's why Jesus asked the invalid, "Do you want to be well?" Maybe that's why you can sense his Spirit asking you the same question. Do you want to enjoy the benefits of technology without being ensnared by the curses? Do you really want to change? Do you really want to be well?

Because you can't help someone who *needs* help.

You can only help someone who *wants* help.

Do you want to be free?

You have to want it. Really want it.

The healing will not begin until your desire is greater than your disability.

When you finally realize that you want to be well more than you want to be wired, then you've opened the door for God to work in your life. If you're tired of surfing, trying to fill the hole in your heart that only Jesus can fill, then it's time for healing. If you're sick of being a slave to the latest operating system or to having a Wi-Fi connection at a restaurant, and you're ready to do something about it, then you've taken your first step.

THE POWER TO CHANGE

Addictions are rarely easy to overcome. But God will start the healing process if you let him, if you're willing to rely on his power to do what you cannot do on your own.

My dad is the perfect example. He was addicted to alcohol for much of my life. Every night I was at home as a child and we were alone, I remember my dad drinking. *Every night.* Then when he was fifty-one years old, something clicked in him. Something snapped. Something changed. Dad had had enough. He was ready to change. He surrendered his addiction to God and asked for help. As his relationship with God grew, so did Dad's desire to get well. He admitted that he had a problem, and he decided to do whatever it took to get help.

My dad has now been sober for more than twenty-three years, for which he gives Jesus all the credit. Now he helps others get free of their addictions and devotes much of his time to a prison ministry and serving on the board of two nonprofits focused on recovery for addicts. The change makes me emotional as I write this. I could not be more proud and thankful for God's work in his life.

One day I was wondering how long he'd been hooked, so I asked him, "Dad, I know when you stopped drinking, but when did you start?"

He paused to reflect. "Well, I guess I was . . ." I could tell he was trying to remember. "I think I was thirteen years old."

Since I didn't pay a lot of attention in math (we already established that), I opened my handy calculator app. How long did my dad have a problem? Let's see, fifty-one (the age he stopped) minus thirteen (the age he started) should equal the number of years he was addicted.

Thirty-eight years. Just like the guy in John's gospel.

There's nothing magical about that number. It was only when Dad's desire for healing became greater than his disability that God began to set him free. And after thirty-eight years, by the power of Christ, my dad became free.

Maybe you are addicted, hooked, and have been struggling to be free for some time. I don't know how long you've been down, but with Christ you're not out.

It's time to stop making excuses and start getting well. When he looked at the crippled man, "Jesus said to him, '*Get up! Pick up your mat and walk.*' At once the man was cured; he picked up his mat and walked" (John 5:8–9, emphasis added). Jesus didn't heal the man a month later; it happened *immediately*. In the same way, when you surrender this challenge to Jesus, he can do more in that moment than you can even imagine. You might not feel any different, and the change might not happen all at once, but Jesus' power will be working in you.

Jesus told the invalid to get up and start walking. That's a pretty hefty assignment for a guy who most likely had never walked in his life. Jesus told him to do what everyone else would have considered impossible.

Notice that the guy didn't even ask Jesus to heal him. Jesus just did it because he's Jesus. When you get close to Jesus, he will do things you don't even ask him to do. He's just that good.

Jesus essentially said, "I don't want to hear your excuses. I want to see your faith."

And there you have it. Maybe that's exactly what he's saying to you right now through this book. If you've read this far, then I'm guessing something here is hitting close to home for you.

Right now Jesus may be saying to you, "I don't want to hear your excuses. I want you to believe that I have something even better, something richer for you. Something that will satisfy your longing that nothing else can quench."

> **When you get close to Jesus, he will do things you don't even ask him to do. He's just that good.**

I don't know what this will look like in your life, but if you're serious about getting well, God will show you. You might take a three-day break from technology, just to see if you can leave it alone. Or you might break from it for thirty days for a deeper detox. If technology or social media has become an idol for you, God might lead you to close some accounts, delete some apps, or install some filters before you go on with life. I don't know what form breaking this idol will take for you, but you are not what you tweet. Your self-worth is not based on the Likes of others but on the love of God.

When this idol is broken, you will not be overcome by comparisons like you may have been before. When Christ becomes all you have, you will realize that Christ is all you need. You won't be afraid of what you're missing out of on a screen because your life will be so full of what matters most. You will live an unfiltered life, removing the veil and sharing your heart intimately. And you will care deeply about people. You won't simply Like posts; you will love people—deeply, from the heart.

When you occasionally (or often) unplug, you will find true rest for your soul. When you make pleasant boundaries, you will be making wise choices to keep your eyes, mind, and heart pure. You will not put anything ahead of God. When others are tempted to tear people down, you will break from the crowd and follow God, who has called you to build others up.

As you remove the blanket of excuses and follow God's leading, you will contemplate the glory of God and be transformed into the image of Christ, because you are defined not by who follows you but by whom you follow.

Do you want to get well?

Then let Jesus heal you.

He is more powerful than any #struggles you will ever face.

THE TEN COMMANDMENTS OF USING SOCIAL MEDIA TO GROW YOUR FAITH AND SHARE GOD'S LOVE

I don't know about you, but the word *holy* can be intimidating.

But *holy* is definitely a word closely associated with God. It's part of how we describe him, and how he describes himself. We first see the concept of holiness applied to people shortly after God delivered the Israelites from bondage in Egypt. As they traveled through the desert and made camp near Mount Sinai (also known as Mount Horeb), they discovered how God wanted them to act based on who they were. God rescued the Israelites to become a holy nation, a people set apart to glorify him.

In the same way, through Jesus, God has called us to be holy (1 Peter 2:9).

To be holy means to be set apart, to be different. The good news is that we are not made holy by our good behavior or by our own righteousness. We are made holy by the righteousness of God through his sinless Son, Jesus. As Paul explains, "God made him who had no sin to be sin for us, so that in him we might become the righteousness of God" (2 Cor. 5:21). Because Jesus was without sin, he could die in our place as a sacrifice for our sins.

When we put our faith in Jesus, his death and resurrection make us righteous before God. Somehow we often forget this essential truth: our righteousness, our holiness, is based not on our good works but on our faith. It's a gift given freely so that we can have eternal life with God. "This righteousness is given through faith in Jesus Christ to all who believe" (Rom. 3:22).

In the Old Testament, when God saved his people out of bondage, he saved them for a purpose. God led Moses to the top of Mount Sinai for forty days. During this time, God not only gave Moses detailed instructions for the tabernacle; he also gave Moses two stone tablets inscribed with special instructions we know as the Ten Commandments. Out of his love for his people, God gave them these moral and spiritual laws to keep them safe as well as set them apart.

In the same spirit, I want to suggest ten commandments for you to consider as you use social media. It's pretty obvious these didn't come directly from God. But the principles are definitely based on his Word.

We've spent quite a few pages exploring some of the harmful effects of technology and social media, but let me say again how much I appreciate the amazing benefits of living in a Wi-Fi world. So I want to leave you with these ten ways to protect your time, your heart, your body, and your soul, as well as deepen your faith through what you type, text, and tweet.

These are simply ten helpful suggestions for how you can use social media in ways that will show others your love for God while not allowing social media to define you or to take an unhealthy place in your life. Social media and technology are amazing tools, and with a little discipline and prayer, they can be a gift to connect with others and reflect your love for an amazing God. So just imagine they're on virtual stone tablets, and let's take a look at each one.

1. Put God first in all you say and post.
2. Love others as you want to be loved.
3. Use social media to facilitate, not replace, real relationships.
4. Use social media instead of being controlled by it as an idol.
5. Turn your virtual other cheek to posts that offend you.
6. Do not post out of emotion

7. Always reflect Jesus, loving God whether online or off.

8. Do not use social media to fuel temptations.

9. Form your own opinions; do not follow the crowd.

10. Do not base your identity on what people think.

1. Put God First in All You Say and Post

Sounds easy enough, right? But if it really were that easy, you wouldn't need this book! So let's think about ways you can remind yourself of what is fundamentally true.

When my wife, Amy, was a teenager, her dad always told her before she went out with friends, "Remember *who* you are and *whose* you are." You don't just represent yourself or your family; you represent Christ. Paul says it clearly: "And whatever you do, whether in word or deed, do it all in the name of the Lord Jesus, giving thanks to God the Father through him" (Col. 3:17).

Too often we want to compartmentalize our lives. We're tempted to think we're okay because we do the church thing on Sundays. Then during the week, we do the work thing, and on the weekends, we do our own thing. But in reality, because our lives belong to God, everything we do should be God things. Everything.

He should be first in all we do. If we're watching television, going to the grocery store, studying for an exam, asking someone out on a date, updating our Facebook status, or tweeting about our latest business deal, whatever we do, we should do it for God. Notice the way Paul qualifies his instructions: "whether in word or deed." Whether we're speaking or acting, shouting or singing, do it all for the glory of God. We could translate this into our social-media culture by saying, "Whatever you do, whether tweeting, commenting, posting, or uploading, do it all in the name of the Lord Jesus."

Before saying anything online (or in person), ask yourself whether you are truly representing and reflecting the love and goodness of God. If not, don't say it. Ever. And don't just think about the words you say; think about the pictures or videos you post. If in any way they don't reflect God's standards, don't share them.

I love the way the Living Bible translates Proverbs 3:6. This should be our standard online: "In everything you do, put God first, and he will direct you and crown your efforts with success."

In other words, "Thou shalt put God first in all you say or post."

2. Love Others as You Want to Be Loved

You've probably heard the Golden Rule before: "Do to others as you would have them do to you" (Luke 6:31). Jesus summarized his instruction on how to treat other people with this rule when a group asked him how they should respond to their enemies. Raising the bar higher than ever before, this rule applies when we interact with others in person as well as online.

When you think about how you like to be loved online, it's easy to know how to treat others. For starters is the obvious. You can Like someone's post. You can retweet what they say or reply with a kind word or two. You can offer a sincere and uplifting compliment. You can comment positively on something they said or posted.

You can refrain from saying something hurtful to others, being antagonistic, or always ignoring what they do or say. As a general rule, I try not to post things that are negative and critical. Enough people are doing that. I want what I say and show to be uplifting and encouraging, to build up rather than to tear down. This doesn't mean that we avoid tough issues, but we can talk about them from a positive perspective, offering solutions rather than poking at people and making others look bad.

Besides saying nice things and avoiding ugly online interactions, you can find all kinds of ways to love people using technology and social media. You can take the relationship out of the virtual realm by replying in person. Instead of simply posting a comment, you can reply with a call, a handwritten note, or a personal visit. If someone asks for prayer, you can go to their home and pray with them instead of just praying from a distance. If someone loses a job, you can offer to pay a bill while they're looking for work or help them network to find new job opportunities. And when they get a job, you can go out to dinner with them to celebrate the blessing. You know tons of things that people do for you that help you feel loved. So get creative online and off and love others in the same ways you want to be loved!

3. Use Social Media to Facilitate, Not Replace, Real Relationships

Ten years ago, most of us would have never imagined all the social benefits technology now offers. Even as I'm writing this, I can't believe that I can FaceTime my friends who are halfway around the world or send a text to my daughter who is in the next room. By the time this book is in print, who knows what new forms of social media and technology will have been developed that offer even more ways to stay in touch with those we love or to follow those we admire.

We should maximize all that technology offers to help strengthen our friendships and relationships. But as the gravitational pull to live online continues to grow, we must remind ourselves that the best relationships are not those that are limited to looking at a screen but those that involve loving a person in person.

So text away. Tweet what you're doing. Post what you're eating. But put more effort into your treasured relationships. Remember to call. Plan a visit. Eat with someone, and then sit and chat for two hours afterward. Sit across from each other in a coffee shop and talk about everything that matters and a few things that don't. Make a meal for someone and bring it to their house. Take a long walk with a friend and just chat about whatever comes to mind. When someone you love is injured and in the hospital, don't just text them; go visit them. Don't just do life together from a distance. Do life up close. As Paul might have tweeted, "Be devoted to one another in love" (Rom. 12:10).

4. Use Social Media Instead of Being Controlled by It as an Idol

As followers of Jesus, we need to make sure a good thing never becomes a supreme thing. Unquestionably, leveraging technology to share about Jesus and connect with people is a good thing. But if left unchecked, using technology can become obsessive and idolatrous.

We all know people who are obsessed with how many followers they have, how many have started following them, and who has unfollowed them. Most of us have found ourselves hitting refresh a few too many times in the hope of finding new Likes and comments. Some people get lost in a world of creeping on others, constantly obsessing over what they post or say, sometimes with people they don't even know! Some can't control the urge to look at just one more thing on Pinterest, knowing that one final click (which is never just one) might hold that special something that will finally make their life complete. Still others play just one more game, hoping this time they'll finally break their high score or reach a new level.

It's hard to see it in the moment, but when we stand back, we realize that we might as well have bowed down before a giant smart phone in the sky. The Bible couldn't be clearer about idolatry. In addition to the commandment to "have no other gods before me" (Ex. 20:3), we're also told: "Dear children, keep yourselves from idols" (1 John 5:21). The moment you realize you're starting to put something above God, tear that idol down. As soon as you realize that you don't have control, that you click and click again without knowing how to stop, acknowledge the problem. Don't rationalize it. Don't explain it away. And don't put off dealing with it.

Just tell the truth.

You are addicted.

And it is idolatry.

Once you acknowledge your problem before God, you can ask for his forgiveness and his help. God always hears the prayer of the repentant heart.

Not only will he forgive you, but he will also give you the strength to put away the things that keep you from him.

Use social media. Enjoy it. But don't let it overtake you. If you see an iDol in your life, smash it!

5. Turn Your Virtual Other Cheek to Posts That Offend You

Follow enough people, and it won't take long: someone will say or show something inappropriate or offensive. If you're like most people, you find it easy to get up in arms and take offense. As Christians, though, we can rise above the temptation to get down in the dirt. Solomon says, "A person's wisdom yields patience; it is to one's glory to *overlook an offense*" (Prov. 19:11, emphasis added).

In our culture, many people are quick to judge, quick to call a foul, and quick to be offended. But even though they may be quick to get upset, they're slow to show grace by overlooking offenses. God's Word teaches us to be different from the world. It's to our glory to overlook an offense.

To be clear, overlooking an offense isn't the same as pretending it didn't happen or encouraging injustice. No, to overlook something is a decision to let it go. It's a form of forgiveness. The Hebrew word translated *overlook* also means "to pass over." You can look at what can hurt you and spiritually soar right on by it.

If people say something harsh or sharp, instead of puffing up and striking back, allow God's Spirit to help you give them the benefit of the doubt. Chances are their bad mood isn't about you, and their critical spirit probably isn't against you as much as it's a reflection of something they're dealing with. That someone is constantly angry or harsh is often a sign they're hurting. Why? Because hurting people hurt people. Rather than taking an offense, you should take them to prayer and ask God to help them.

If a post starts to grieve your heart or make you unrighteously angry, remember that you don't have to follow the poster. You can to some degree control what you see and read. No matter what, remember that just as Jesus taught us to turn the other cheek when someone strikes us, so we can turn a virtual other cheek to posts that offend us. Life is too short to allow someone else's bad attitude to pollute our heart and relationships.

6. Do Not Post out of Emotion

When you think about it, the ability to say whatever you're thinking to a large group of semi-interested people is pretty scary, which is a good reason never to post when you're feeling angry, upset, rejected, or offended or are battling any other unsettling emotion. If you're wondering whether you are responding out of emotion, remember this: when in doubt, wait it out.

As a rule, I never, ever post when I'm overly emotional. Never. I have the discipline not to defend myself or get into unnecessary online controversy. For years I've avoided responding to critics or posting out of emotion. Recently, though, I was milliseconds away from breaking my longstanding rule. Our local newspaper took an unfortunate shot at a local professional athlete who also happens to be a friend of mine. Within minutes, it seemed like the majority of our city was in an uproar, leaping to social media to vent their frustrations. Like many, I was angry and hurt on behalf of my friend, who has been a tremendous blessing to our city. So in a fit of righteous anger, I typed out a harsh tweet to defend him. Thankfully, by the grace of God, I hesitated just long enough to think, "Should I post this?" At least 99.5 percent of me wanted to let it fly. But since I was not 100 percent sure, I submitted to my default rule: when in doubt, wait it out.

I am so thankful that I didn't take a shot at our local media. They have been really fair in their reporting about our church and are often generous. Whatever I said wouldn't have changed what they had already said about my friend. And within time, the writer apologized for his sloppy comment. The management of the publication also seemed genuinely sorry and embarrassed. The entire controversy blew over in a few days. Had I posted, I might have felt better in the moment, but it wouldn't have helped anyone. I know I've made more than my share of mistakes, so I'm glad that instead of shooting at someone in that moment, I managed to stay out of the crossfire.

Without a doubt, you will be tempted to post when you're agitated or hurt. But when in doubt, wait it out. Post only out of love.

7. Always Reflect Jesus, Loving God Whether Online or Off

After Jesus had silenced the attacking Sadducees, the Pharisees conspired to trap him. One of the experts baited Jesus by asking him which commandment was the greatest. "Jesus replied: 'Love the Lord your God with all your heart and with all your soul and with all your mind.' This is the first and greatest commandment" (Matt. 22:37–38). Above all else, the most important command we have is to love God with every part of our being. Therefore, we should always love and reflect Jesus online and off.

I encourage you to go through everything you've posted or said online in the past month. Pretend like you don't know anything about yourself. Look at everything objectively and determine what conclusions someone would draw about you based on what you've posted. Do you like what you see? What does your online footprint reveal about you? Does what you show accurately reflect what you believe? Would people say you love God above all? Or would they think you love something else more—maybe even yourself?

This doesn't mean the only things we ever post should be Bible verses or quotes from your pastor's sermon. But over a month's time, certainly people should be able to see evidence that we love God and follow Jesus. If this evidence is not in your posts, ask yourself why not. Are you afraid of what people will think? Or worse yet, are you revealing that you aren't really loving God above all else?

If you are falling more and more in love with God each day, your love will show in the things you post. You won't have to force it or fake it. If you realize you are forcing or faking it, instead of trying to show something that's not real or genuine, acknowledge that you aren't loving God with all you have and all you are. Ask him to help you, to guide you, and to draw you. When you seek him, you will find him (see Jer. 29:13). He will reveal himself to you. When you experience him and taste his goodness, you will see that he is good (see Ps. 34:8). Once your passion for him grows, so will your online and offline witness for him.

Thou shalt always reflect Jesus.

Love God online and off.

8. Do Not Use Social Media to Fuel Temptations

It's no secret that technology and social media can open the door to temptations with simple clicks or keystrokes. Instead of having to go through numerous steps, actions, or behaviors to come face to face with a fierce temptation, we can now encounter it on our monitors in nanoseconds.

I don't mean just sexual temptations. A shopping app for some is more temptation to click and buy than they can handle on a weak evening with nothing to do. Or an open door to gambling is the worst possible temptation for someone who feels lucky—again. For others, online gossip quietly whispers their name: "Come get in on the know." Some are tempted to compare, to overshare, or to look and lust. It's important to be honest about where you're vulnerable, and plan to avoid the traps that can hurt you.

James, the half-brother of Jesus, doesn't pull punches when he describes the deception and dangers of temptation. After explaining clearly that God never tempts, James adds, "Each person is tempted when they are dragged away by their own evil desire and enticed. Then, after desire has conceived, it gives birth to sin; and sin, when it is full-grown, gives birth to death" (James 1:14–15). The Greek word James uses that is translated *enticed* is actually a fishing term that illustrates how temptation baits us and then hooks us. What starts out as something small and seemingly harmless can quickly become something big and dangerous, even deadly.

However, as a believer in Jesus, you never have to battle temptation alone. The author of Hebrews reminds us that "because [Jesus] himself suffered when he was tempted, he is able to help those who are being tempted" (Heb. 2:18). If you are being tempted, you are not on your own. Jesus is able to help you. So if you spot an open door to online temptation, ask Jesus to help you close it.

When you pray for wisdom, God will give it to you (see James 1:5). When he shows you how to shut the door to online temptation, slam that door, lock it, and throw away the encryption key. Delete the app if you have to. Or if you need to, give someone else a password to keep yourself from having access to download apps. You might need to download a filtered browser or block certain websites. (Find more explanation on how to do all of these things in appendix 2.) Or you might share passwords or have joint accounts with your spouse. Whatever it takes, thou shalt not use technology to fuel temptation.

9. Form Your Own Opinions; Do Not Follow the Crowd

When you follow other people online, you can learn a lot of wisdom from those who are wise. Unfortunately, not only are some people not wise, they can be downright foolish. Proverbs 15:2 says, "The tongue of the wise adorns knowledge, but the mouth of the fool gushes folly." I love the way the New Living Translation translates the last part of this verse. It says, "the mouth of a fool belches out foolishness." Chances are you've seen this type of person let loose online.

Jesus instructs us to stay on the narrow road, warning that the broad or wide road leads to destruction (see Matt. 7:13–14). Sometimes it seems as if everyone is going the same way, but that doesn't mean they are going the right way. Often on social media, many people jump on the bandwagons of opinions about God, politics, or the latest celebrity scandal. But just because a lot of people believe something doesn't make it true. Especially when it comes to what people post online.

It may be tempting to follow the crowd, but doing so can be dangerous. Exodus 23:2 says, "Do not follow the crowd in doing wrong." God gave you a brain to think for yourself. He gave you his Word to seek his will. He gave you his Spirit to guide you into all truth (see John 16:13). Instead of believing everything you see or hear, think for yourself.

Paul explains the importance of resisting the lure of the crowd when he says, "Do not conform to the pattern of this world" (Rom. 12:2). Don't be like everyone else. The Message loosely translates this same verse: "Don't become so well-adjusted to your culture that you fit into it without even thinking." Instead of doing what most everyone else does or believing what many say is true, we should have our minds renewed by God's truth.

Resist the urge to blend in.

Don't be a sheep and follow the herd.

Follow the Shepherd.

10. Do Not Base Your Identity on What People Think

Anyone who spends time on social media will be tempted to compare, thinking, "How many followers do they have? Wow! That's way more than I have." We may also be tempted to think the opposite when we see that someone gets fewer Likes or mentions than we do—that they aren't as important as we are. An unhealthy view of social media can cause us to feel either an ungodly pride or an unhealthy sense of inadequacy.

Not only can we be tempted to base our identity on who follows us (or by who doesn't), but we can also allow ourselves to be consumed by what others say. If they Like our new shirt in our latest selfie, we feel great. If they don't say anything, we might assume they don't like it. And if they say, "What were u thinkin when u bought that UGLY thang?" we might never shop at the same store again.

As Christians, we must constantly remind ourselves not to base our identity—our view of ourselves and our worth—on what other people say or think about us. Who we are and our value is determined by what Christ says about us. Others may criticize us, ignore us, or unfollow us, but that doesn't affect who we really are. We are who Christ says we are.

In case you're wondering what he says about you, here's a short list. You are a new creation (2 Cor. 5:17). You are forgiven, and your sins are washed away (Eph. 1:7). You are more than a conqueror (Rom. 8:37). You are God's masterpiece (Eph. 2:10 NLT).

I could go on. "You are the light of the world" (Matt. 5:14). You are filled with the same spirit that raised Christ from the dead (Rom. 8:11). You are a joint heir with Christ (Rom. 8:17). You are Christ's divine representative to this world (2 Cor. 5:20). You are the righteousness of God in Christ (2 Cor. 5:21). You are greatly loved by God (John 14:20–23).

No matter what anyone says or implies, you do not need to be moved by their words. You are secure in Christ and Christ alone. Thou shalt not base your identity on what people think.

So there you have the ten commandments for using social media. It can be tempting to view these like we often view the Ten Commandments that God gave Moses—as burdens that limit what we can and can't do. But in truth, God's commandments are supreme blessings that free us to serve him faithfully and to live joyfully. In the same way, I pray these ten commandments of social media will provide love-giving and life-protecting boundaries that enable you to enjoy relating to others online without losing focus on what matters most.

So post, tweet, click, snap, text, chat, comment, and enjoy it all. But do it all out of the overflow of your love for God and love for people. Use technology, but don't let it overtake your life. Enjoy the benefits of technology, but don't let it define you.

Whatever you do, do it all for the glory of God.

Appendix 2

SAFEGUARDS

As we've discussed throughout this book, you may want to limit access to certain sites, apps, or information for a number of reasons. For example, you may want to shield a child from the wrong types of online influences or keep them from wasting time on useless games. You may honestly acknowledge that you can't seem to keep yourself from looking at something inappropriate and prefer not to have access. Or you may be addicted to an app or a site and want to eliminate all access to something that is holding you captive.

Here are a few safeguards to help you distance yourself from online temptations or distractions. These suggestions obviously are not comprehensive, but they do provide a starting point for protecting yourself and those you love.

Your Computer

If you want to protect yourself or others from dangerous temptations on your computer, consider an internet filter. These are easy to install and often free. Among many great choices, here are a few to consider:

- K9 Web Protection
- Integrity Online
- Accountable2You

- Saavi Accountability
- SafePlace.Net
- XXXChurch.com
- Covenant Eyes

Your iPhone and iPad

Here are some ways to eliminate online distractions and temptations. You may or may not need all of these, but I'll suggest the most extreme safeguards, and you can decide which are most appropriate for yourself or those you care about.

First, you'll want to either block Safari and use a filtered web browser app, or put safeguards into place for Safari, or both.

Here are the steps to block Safari:

1. Go into Settings.
2. Tap "General."
3. Scroll down and tap "Restrictions."
4. Tap "Enable Restrictions" and create a four-digit passcode two times, entering it twice. If you want this blocked for yourself, have someone else create the passcode and not tell you what it is.
5. Now you can scroll down and block access to Safari and other apps, turn off options such as the ability to install apps, and set the ratings for music, movies, TV shows, books, and apps.

If you are blocking Safari, you should also consider blocking the ability to download apps, since many seemingly innocent social media apps include easy access to porn, filthy language, and plenty of other harmful content. If you hold the four-digit passcode, then you are the only one who can determine which apps your child or others can access.

If you choose to block Safari but still want access to the internet, then download an app designed to block inappropriate content. There are many good ones to choose from. Based on recommendations from friends and my own use, I recommend:

- Mobicip
- K9 Web Protection
- X3 Watch
- Ranger Pro Safe Browser

If you are concerned about a child seeing inappropriate content, I strongly recommend that you block adult content on Safari even if you use a filtered browser app. Many people don't know that you can click on an advertisement on many apps, and the ad will give you total access to the internet. Blocking adult content offers more protection for a child who may know more about how to get internet access than you do.

If you want to use Safari but limit adult content or block certain sites, follow these steps:

1. Go into Settings.
2. Tap "General."
3. Scroll down and tap on "Restrictions."
4. If you have already enabled restrictions, you will need to enter the passcode. If you have not, then tap "Enable Restrictions" and create a passcode, entering it two times.
5. Scroll down to "Allowed Content."
6. Tap "Websites."
7. Tap "Limit Adult Content."
8. If you want to never allow particular websites, you can add them to your list. Or if you want to allow only a few websites for a child and nothing else, tap on "Specific Websites Only" and choose which websites to allow.

Your Android Phone

These steps are excerpted from *PCAdvisor.co.uk*.[25]

Step 1. From the Android home screen, pull down from the top right and tap on Settings. Scroll down to and select Users, then tap 'Add user or profile'. You can create either a normal User profile, or a Restricted profile. Tap on the latter.

Step 2. If you haven't done so already, you'll be prompted to set up a screen lock for your device. Tap Set lock, then choose to use either a pattern, PIN or password lock and follow the instructions.

Step 3. Tap the settings icon next to the 'New profile' to give it a name.

Step 4. You'll now see a list of apps installed on your device, with on/off toggles to the side. By default, the restricted profile is unable to access any of these. Go through the list and toggle on only the apps you are comfortable with your child accessing. The list includes any web browsers installed on your tablet, so leave these switched to off if you're worried about what harm your child may come to online. You can also click on the Settings icon next to Settings to allow apps to use location information, which is switched off by default.

Step 5. From the lock screen, you'll now find your own account is protected with a pattern, password or PIN, while your child can instantly access their own account—but only the apps you deem appropriate. Although the Google Play Store icon appears, trying to access this will bring up a notification that you do not have permission to use the Google Play Store.

Your Television

If you are concerned about yourself or loved ones seeing harmful images on cable or satellite TV, find out online or from your provider how to block programs with certain ratings or content. I have blocked the ability to order movies on my TVs and blocked access to certain ratings to protect my young children.

Final Thoughts

If we didn't cover something in this brief appendix that concerns you, you can probably find help online by googling the information you need. If you are more of a visual learner, you can often find video instructions on YouTube that will show you how to do the things we covered here and more.

Remember, God offers help: "No temptation has overtaken you except what is common to mankind. And God is faithful; he will not let you be tempted beyond what you can bear. But when you are tempted, he will also provide a way out so that you can endure it" (1 Cor. 10:13).

ACKNOWLEDGMENTS

I'd like to express my deepest gratitude to all my friends who helped make this book possible.

Dudley Delffs, you are the best editor I know. And you are an even better friend.

David Morris, Tom Dean, John Raymond, Brian Phipps, Lisa Eary, and the whole team at Zondervan, it's truly an honor to publish with you. Your passion to glorify Christ shows and means more to me than I can ever express.

Tom Winters, thank you for always representing me well. You are a faithful friend.

Brannon Golden, you're a genius and a comedian. Thanks for always making time to do your *thang!* You're the best of the best.

Lori Tapp and Adrianne Manning, you are both rock stars. Thank you for serving my family and making our world better.

Mandy Groeschel, Cindy Beall, Jaclyn Vann, Jared Bowie, Blake Deprato, and Michael Mead, thank you for reading through the manuscript and offering your valuable feedback. You made the book stronger. And because of you, there are no pics in the book.

Catie, Mandy, Anna, Sam, Stephen, Joy, you didn't really do a lot to help with this book, but since you are my kids and I'm crazy about you, I put your names in the acknowledgments. I am proud of each of you and love you more than you can imagine.

Amy Groeschel, you are better than words can describe. I love life with you. You are my best friend and my dream girl forever.

NOTES

1. Allan Hall, "Facebook 'Makes You Feel Miserable and Jealous,'" *DailyMail.com*, January 22, 2013, *http://www.dailymail.co.uk/sciencetech/article-2266317/Unsociable -networking-Researchers-say-checking-Facebook-make-miserable-jealous.html*.

2. Aaron Smith, "Six New Facts About Facebook," Pew Research Center *Fact Tank*, February 3, 2014, *http://www.pewresearch.org/ fact-tank/2014/02/03/6-new-facts-about-facebook/*.

3. Janet Kornblum, "Study: 25% of Americans Have No One to Confide In," *USA Today*, June 22, 2006, *http://usatoday30.usatoday.com/news/nation/2006-06-22- friendship_x.htm*.

4. Ibid.

5. Shea Bennett, "The #Selfie Phenomenon," *Social Times*, October 17, 2013, *http:// www.mediabistro.com/alltwitter/the-selfie-phenomenon_b50630*.

6. Ibid.

7. Chris Gayomali, "Are Selfies Fueling a Plastic Surgery Boom?" *Fast Company*, December 2, 2014, *http://www.fastcompany.com/3039208/ are-selfies-fueling-a-plastic-surgery-boom?partner=rss*.

8. Sara H. Konrath, Edward H. O'Brien, and Courtney Hsing, "Changes in Dispositional Empathy in American College Students Over Time: A Meta-Analysis," Personality and Social Psychology Review 15, no. 2 (2011): 180–98, *http://www .sitemaker.umich.edu/eob/files/konrathetal2011.pdf*.

9. Courtney Seiter, "Seven Social Media Psychology Studies That Will Make Your Marketing Smarter," blog post, August 13, 2014, *https://blog.bufferapp.com/ social-media-psychology-studies-smarter-marketing*.

10. Robert Weiss, "The Prevalence of Porn," *Sex and Intimacy in the Digital Age*, n.d., *http://blogs.psychcentral.com/sex/2013/05/the-prevalence-of-porn/*.

11. Pam Spaulding, "Christian Women Increasingly Suffering from Sexual Addiction," *AlterNet*, October 17, 2007, *http://www.alternet.org/story/65469/ christian_women_increasingly_suffering_from_sexual_addiction*.

12. Danielle Tiano, "Statistics," Temptation of a Generation, n.d., *http://www .temptationseries.com/statistics.html*.

13. Quentin Fottrell, "Does Facebook Break Up Marriages?" *MarketWatch*, July 13, 2014, *http://www.marketwatch.com/story/does-facebook-break-up-marriages-2014-07-07*.

14. Daniel Weiss, "Pornography U.: Emerging Adults and Pornography Use," *Rock*, April 6, 2011, *http://www.myrocktoday.org/default.asp?q_areaprimaryid=7&q_areasecondaryid =74&q_areatertiaryid=0&q_articleid=860*.

15. "Cyber Bullying Statistics 2014," *NoBullying.com*, last modified February 11, 2015, *http://nobullying.com/cyber-bullying-statistics-2014/*.

16. Cavan Sieczkowski, "Family Denies Writing Anti-Gay Message on Receipt for Waitress Dayna Morales, Claims It's a Hoax," *Huffington Post*, November 26, 2013, *http://www .huffingtonpost.com/2013/11/26/family-anti-gay-receipt-hoax_n_4343563.html*.

17. Pamela B. Rutledge, "Making Sense of Selfies," *PsychcologyToday.com*, July 6, 2013, *https://www.psychologytoday.com/blog/positively-media/201307/making-sense-selfies*.

18. Rebecca Savastio, "Selfies Cause Narcissism, Mental Illness, Addiction, and Suicide?" April 8, 2014, *Guardian Liberty Voice*, *http://guardianlv.com/2014/04/ selfies-cause-narcissism-mental-illness-addiction-and-suicide/*.

19. Tim Elmore, "Nomophobia: A Rising Trend in Students," *GrowingLeaders.com*, September 2, 2014, *http://growingleaders.com/blog/new-trend-students-nomophobia/*.

20. Ibid.

21. Eddie Wrenn, "The Biggest Phobia in the World? 'Nomophobia'—the Fear of Being without Your Mobile—Affects 66 Percent of Us," *DailyMail.com*, *http://www .dailymail.co.uk/sciencetech/article-2141169/The-biggest-phobia-world-Nomophobia-- fear-mobile--affects-66-cent-us.html*. These studies were done in the UK but probably also reflect American attitudes.

22. Ibid.

23. Connie Loizos, "Eighty-Seven Percent of Teens Sleep with Their Cell Phones and Other Alarming Statistics," *PEHub.com*, April 20, 2010, *https://www.pehub .com/2010/04/87-percent-of-teens-sleep-with-their-cell-phones-and-other-alarming -statistics/*.

24. Meena Hart Duerson, "We're Addicted to Our Phones," *New York Daily News*, August 16, 2012, *http://www.nydailynews.com/life-style/ addicted-phones-84-worldwide-couldn-single-day-mobile-device-hand-article-1.1137811*.

25. Marie Brewis, "How to Set Up Parental Control on Android: Restrict Android App Permissions," *PCAdvisor.co.uk*, March 2, 2015, *http://www.pcadvisor.co.uk/how-to/ google-android/3461359/parental-control-on-android/*.

An excerpt from Craig Groeschel's next book,
Divine Direction: 7 Decisions That Will Change Your Life:

Chapter 1

START

Nobody can go back and start a new beginning, but
anyone can start today and make a new ending.

Maria Robinson

She dragged the wet clothes from the washer into a basket to carry them out to the line in the back yard. As the morning summer sun kept inching higher, she knew it wouldn't take long for them to dry. She also knew it wouldn't take long for her little house to heat up like an oven. Which meant she'd better get to that ironing before it got any hotter.

She had set up her ironing board on her little screened-in porch, both for the shade and for the hope of a stray breeze here and there. She sifted through the clean, dry stack from an earlier load and selected a blue Oxford dress shirt, monogramed with the initials of a local banker. He was a good man, one of her best clients. She took great pride in her work, determined to make a difference in her customers' lives by helping them look their best in fresh, spotless, perfectly pressed shirts, pants, and dresses.

As she ironed, she smiled to herself, recalling a conversation she'd had the previous week with the banker while he was wearing this blue shirt. She had gone in that day to deposit a little money into her savings account, and the banker had greeted her like family. He invited her to take a seat while he looked over her accounts.

After a minute, he let out a long, low whistle. "Why, Ms. McCarty, you have more money in this bank than I do! Don't you ever spend any of it on yourself?"

She laughed and shook her head. "There's nothin' I need. God is good to me, and he provides everything I could ever want. No sir, I'm savin' my money for a special purpose he's laid on my heart."

"And what would that be?" he asked. The banker was like most people, expecting Ms. McCarty to say she hoped for a bigger house or a cruise or maybe a shopping spree in Memphis or Atlanta.

"Well, I want to set up a scholarship fund at the university for young people who can't afford to go there. I never was able to get an education myself, but I sure do appreciate the value of one. And I want to help some young women and men have that opportunity I never got."

The memory faded as she turned the shirt over and over, carefully smoothing it with the steaming iron. She had started saving pennies and nickels and dimes as a little girl, and by the time she was a young woman, she was saving whole dollars. She had worked as a laundress most of her life, washing and ironing other people's clothes from all over Hattiesburg. Oseola knew her nature was frugal, but she also knew her habit of saving just a little each week would make a profound difference in people's lives long after she left this earth to be with the Lord.

She chuckled to herself, content in the pleasure she found in using her small habit to touch people she would never meet. She folded the blue shirt, humming an old gospel hymn as she set it aside and lifted out the next one.

1.1 WHAT'S YOUR STORY?

In the beginning . . .

Once upon a time . . .

It was a dark and stormy night . . .

Everyone's story has a unique beginning. My story started differently than yours, and yours began differently than everyone else's. But regardless of how our stories began, each of us lives out the story of our life every day.

If you're like me, you don't stop very often to think about "the story of your life." You're too busy living it! But recognizing the pattern of events in your life, the ebbs and flows of your own story, can make a huge difference, both in your future and in how your story ends. Because when you understand the negative ways your past may be influencing your present, you have the power to make different choices, better choices. Thoughtful reflection may also give you a clearer understanding about which things in your life you can change and which things you can't. These are our best decisions ever.

If someone asked you to tell your story, what would you say? You might start with where you were born and how you were raised. You'd describe your favorite teacher, your first crush, your first car. You might include that time you scored the winning touchdown or that *other* time you threw up right before singing your first solo. Maybe you'd mention the big move your family made or when you left home to go to college. If you're married, you might describe how you met your spouse. And if you're not married, you might describe the kind of person you hope to meet one day. If you're a parent, you might scroll through some photos on your phone or tablet and show off your family. Or maybe you'd discuss your latest promotion at work or when you hope to finally launch your own business.

Most of what you tell other people probably sounds pretty good. Maybe you're proud of your story. You've overcome some obstacles. You've survived some challenges. You've accomplished some goals.

Sure, you haven't been perfect or lived a flawless life, but who has? You've made your share of mistakes. (Lord knows, we all have.) Some decisions you got right, and others . . . well, let's just say they're not as easy to discuss. You've had lapses of judgment. If you're like most people, you've made some emotion-based decisions you ended up regretting.

Chances are you might have some chapters in your story that you'd rather not share with anyone. You might have secrets you've never told to another living person. As you reflect back over the course of your years, you might have done things you wish you'd never done.

Maybe you've ended up somewhere you never wanted to be. You didn't mean to blow it, but you did. You made decisions that took you farther than you ever intended to go. You did some things that cost you more than you ever thought you'd have to pay. You hurt people. You compromised your values. You broke personal promises. You did things you can't undo. There's no do-over like when you were a kid on the playground.

Sometimes you simply skip over those dark chapters of your life. Other times you embellish your stories on the fly, adding a few details to make a version you like better than the truth, both to tell yourself and others. You brush past the ugly parts and retell the happier highlights. If you can be honest with yourself, you know that the truth about your story weaves all your decisions together: some good, some not so good, and some still uncertain.

No matter how you would describe your story right now, there's good news. Your story is not over. It's not too late to change the story of your life that you'll tell one day in the future. Regardless of what you've done (or haven't done) in the past, your future is still unwritten. You have more chapters to write, more victories to win, more friends to meet, more of a difference to make, more of God's goodness to experience. Even though you may not like the plot line your life has followed up until now, with God's help, you can still transform your story into one you're not ashamed to share. You can start something new.

While past events cannot be unwritten, they can be redeemed in your chapters to come. No matter how desperate, uncertain, afraid, or stuck you may feel in life right now, your story isn't over. You may think your story is tragic or unbelievable or horrific or boring or funny, but you don't know how it ends. Regardless of whether you think of your story as a tragedy, comedy, fantasy, epic, or something else, it's not too late to change the kind of story you're living.

Your best decision ever is the next one that will help you be the person God created you to be.

1.2 START WHERE YOU ARE

I've heard it said that two of the biggest mistakes you can make in life are not starting and not finishing. If you're like most people, you've had intentions to start some new habits in life. It's a pretty safe bet that many of those good intentions you never followed through on. And it's probably equally likely that even for the things you *did* start, many of those, you never finished. I know what that's like. Regret sets in, and you don't feel successful. You don't feel disciplined. Sometimes you even feel like a failure.

It goes without saying that you can't travel back in time and start your story all over again. But there is something you *can* do, and you can do it today: you can start a new discipline that will make for a new and better ending to your story. Any day you choose, you can start something new and allow God, the finisher of your faith, to help you complete what he called you to start.

So many people think a successful life is made up of just a few big decisions. Starting that new business. Moving to a new city. Inventing an all-new product line. Writing that movie script. Big decisions are important, but a truly meaningful life doesn't happen through a few big decisions; you build it by stacking hundreds and hundreds of smaller ones. Vincent van Gogh nailed it when he said, "Great things are done by a series of small things brought together."

Remember the story I shared at the beginning of this section? Oseola McCarty dropped out of school at an early age and worked most of her life doing other people's laundry in Hattiesburg, Mississippi. As an uneducated African-American woman growing up before the civil rights movement, she had few opportunities for advancement. Her life was incredibly challenging. Yet she savored each day, worked hard, and loved the Lord. During her lifetime she saved more than $150,000, which she donated to create a scholarship fund for financially challenged students at the University of Southern Mississippi. Ms. McCarty's story proves that starting small can lead to a big positive difference in the lives of many people. The example she set shows that a great life is built by small disciplines and wise decisions.

In this section, we're going to prayerfully allow our coauthor, Jesus, to show us what we need to *start* in order to finish well. We'll focus specifically on life-altering disciplines and habits. I'm not going to ask you to think about following your dreams or starting a new life mission. I don't want you to think about starting a business, writing a book, or launching a ministry. We'll get to those types of decisions later.

We're going to start small. But don't be discouraged. Most great ministries start small. Most great businesses had humble beginnings. Even the best marriages usually start with a simple hello. In the Bible, Zechariah says, "Do not despise these small beginnings, for the LORD rejoices to see the work begin" (Zechariah 4:10 NLT).

If you try to focus now on the last chapter of your story, you'll likely find yourself too paralyzed to even start writing the first page. If you try to imagine the end, it seems too grand, so distant, so ideal, that you won't know where to begin. The dream will remain just that: only a dream. That's why we're going to start simple and take just one small step in the direction of the dream.

Let's say you want to tell the story of running a marathon. Can you go out and run one today? Unless you've already been training for months, the answer is no. But you can start to jog (or even walk) twenty minutes a day. That's one small step in the direction of your ultimate story. If you want to preach to thousands of people, can you do that today? Again, it's not likely. But can you write one message a week to learn your way around the Bible? Of course you can! If you want to produce a major motion picture, can you do that by Christmas? No way. But you can start making short films with whatever camera you have or can borrow. You can write at least a few lines in the right direction of your future story.

I like to say it this way: I will do today what I *can* do, to enable me to do tomorrow what I can't do today. I will start whatever habit I can that will take me one step closer to the story I want to tell. Mother Teresa reminded us to be "faithful in the small things because it is in them that your strength lies."

Your best decision ever may seem small, but that doesn't mean it can't have a huge impact.

1.3 FLOSSING AND TURNING

I'm convinced that certain positive disciplines in a person's life usually pave the way for a myriad of other positive disciplines. Certain good habits create other good habits. The opposite is also true. The absence of strategic habits cascades into even more bad habits. An undisciplined life never leads to productivity or progress. If you don't put the right disciplines in place, one day you're going to find yourself telling the story you never wanted to tell.

I was planning on it, but I never got around to it.

I should have tried it, but now it's too late.

I never thought I'd end up here. I wish I could do it all over again.

Why didn't I at least try? Now look where I am in life.

I've taught in leadership settings and in the book *From This Day Forward* what I call the Flossing Principle. To the delight of dental hygienists every-where, I tell people they must never quit flossing. Then I explain how flossing is an essential discipline in my life. Flossing likely won't be as important to you as it is to me. And my message isn't that I want you to have healthy gums. I do, but what I'm trying to convey is that we all have important habits that we must develop and then maintain because they trigger other right behaviors. And their absence triggers wrong behaviors.

Why is flossing so important to me? Because it's the first and easiest discipline for me to quit. I've never liked flossing (probably because I'm some-what rebellious and I hate being told I *have* to do something). One time my dentist quoted back to me my own teaching. "You know, Craig, the decisions you make today determine the story you'll tell tomorrow. What story do you want to tell? One with all your teeth? Or one with rotten gums and your teeth falling out?"

I couldn't argue because he was using my own words against me—and also because he was holding a sharp instrument in my mouth. But that same evening, I started flossing before bed. I still don't enjoy it. When I'm tired, I'd rather just brush my teeth and fall into bed. No harm done, right? But my choosing not to floss opens the door for other challenges.

When I force myself to floss even though I don't want to, I feel disciplined. Since I feel disciplined, I continue with my workout plan. Since I work out, I eat better. I sleep better too. And when I sleep well, I wake up early and do my Bible reading before work. Then I go to work in a good frame of mind and I'm more productive. People applaud my good work, so I come home in a good mood and kiss my wife. And that's why we have six kids together.

On the other hand, when I don't floss, I don't feel disciplined. When I break the momentum of my discipline, I'm more tempted to drop other habits as well. Since I didn't floss, I'm more likely to skip a workout, which then helps me rationalize eating more junk food. Those lazy, sloppy habits then come back to haunt me when I don't sleep as well at night.

I toss and turn all night, then wake up tired, grumpy, and even more apathetic. Since I don't feel well, I skip my Bible study, falling even deeper into my self-made pit. When I'm at work, I'm not in a good frame of mind, so I'm not as productive and I get easily distracted. Since I'm not as focused as usual, I have to work late to get everything done. Knowing Amy won't be happy that I'm late coming home, I speed down back roads, only to be pulled over by a police officer who's waiting patiently for a speeder like me. I don't want to get a speeding ticket, so I try to outrun him, only to be stopped just a block from my home by four other police officers who've set up a roadblock. Then my mug shot ends up on the ten o'clock news, and I spend the night in jail—all because I didn't floss.

Okay, so maybe I'm exaggerating. A little. But you have to agree: certain disciplines lead to other positive actions.

And the path to discipline begins with your next best decision.

1.4 OVERNIGHT SUCCESS

Behind every great story, there's always another story. Rarely does success come without time, discipline, and hard work. Successful people often joke that they spent years becoming an "overnight success." What many don't realize is that it's the things no one sees that result in the things everyone wants. It's the faithfulness to do mundane things well, to develop productive habits, and to remain faithful before the payoff is visible that eventually leads to success.

The Old Testament prophet Daniel is a great example of this. Whether you know a lot or a little about Daniel, when you hear his name, you probably think, "Oh, yeah . . . Daniel in the lions' den." Any kid who grew up attending Sunday school or visiting vacation Bible school has undoubtedly heard the amazing story of Daniel surviving overnight in a cave filled with hungry felines. But there's way more to this great story than meets the eye.

Let me refresh your memory, and then we'll go back to the part many overlook. King Darius was the reigning king of Persia. As his kingdom grew, he appointed 120 satraps (similar to our state governors) to handle regional matters and help govern the people. The king then chose three administrators to oversee those 120 satraps. Daniel was one of the chosen leaders. Over time, by consistently serving the king with an excellent spirit, Daniel stood out among all the other satraps and administrators. Eventually the king decided to place Daniel in charge of the entire kingdom.

So Daniel was an overnight success, right? It looks like he was in the right place at the right time, getting lucky when others didn't fare as well. Surely he must have been born a natural leader.

Actually, nothing could be farther from the truth. Don't forget, there's a story behind every story. Why was Daniel successful? Why was he favored above others? Why did the king respect him so much? Promote him so quickly? Believe in his leadership? Why did God look favorably on Daniel? Why did God close the mouths of the meat-eating lions?

We find our answer in a part of Daniel's story that many people skim past. His divine favor was the result of one small decision Daniel made at one point in his life. We don't know when Daniel made this decision or why. We don't know if someone else helped him or if he decided it on his own. All we know is that Daniel made one decision, starting one habit that helped change his story.

Before we look at what Daniel did, let's pick up where we left off. As you might expect, the other leaders were jealous of this "teacher's pet": "At this, the administrators and the satraps tried to find grounds for charges against Daniel in his conduct of government affairs, but they were unable to do so. They could find no corruption in him, because he was trustworthy and neither corrupt nor negligent. Finally these men said, 'We will never find any basis for charges against this man Daniel unless it has something to do with the law of his God'" (Dan. 6:4–5).

Let's pause for a moment and consider some of the great qualities of our hero, Daniel. Even though the other guys did everything they could to find something wrong with him, they couldn't find anything. Daniel was honest, trustworthy, and dependable in all that he did. He was exactly the type of person the king was looking to promote. So his opponents decided there was only one way they could trap Daniel into doing something worthy of punishment. They needed to devise a plan that revolved around his faith in God. They knew he wouldn't do anything wrong. They were going to have to trick him by backing him into a spiritual corner.

"So the administrators and the satraps went as a group to the king and said: 'O King Darius, live forever! The royal administrators, prefects, satraps, advisers and governors have all agreed that the king should issue an edict and enforce the decree that anyone who prays to any god or man during the next thirty days, except to you, O king, shall be thrown into the lions' den'" (vv. 6–8). The king apparently liked the sound of their plan, because he agreed to their proposal. No one could pray to anyone but him for the next month. And so the plan to trap Daniel was set in motion.

We all know what happens next, right? Dan the Man has to stare down the big cats and prove that God is his one and only. But think for a minute. It wasn't just that Daniel wasn't afraid of lions or had some supercourage that mere mortals can never hope to attain. No, Daniel had started a regular practice much earlier in his life that helped him face this impossible situation.

What was it? What secret did he have that helped him live a story worth telling? What discipline helped shape not only what Daniel did but who Daniel was? We find our answers in the next part of his story.

When Daniel heard about the new thirty-day restriction on prayer, he did the same thing he'd done three times a day for months, maybe years, possibly decades. Daniel went to his house and prayed to God.

"Three times a day he got down on his knees and prayed, giving thanks to his God, just as he had done before" (v. 10). In some earlier chapter of Daniel's story, he decided prayer would be a nonnegotiable part of his life. I love that phrase, "as he had done before." We don't know how many years Daniel had been stopping to pray three times a day. But we do know that at some point, Daniel had to have *started* this new discipline. To others, prayer might have seemed small and insignificant. But to Daniel, it was a decision that shaped his story.

Three times a day, every day, Daniel stopped and looked toward heaven. He worshiped God. He aligned his heart to God's heart. He sought God's will to be done through his life. Because of Daniel's consistent and prayerful focus, he grew as a God-follower, as a person, and as a leader.

Unquestionably, that spiritual discipline led to other positive disciplines. And Daniel's faithfulness led to more success, even to the point that the king noticed his exceptional qualities. Daniel wasn't an overnight success. His standing started when he was on his knees. He was able to stand tall because he'd faithfully knelt before the one true King. The small, daily discipline of prayer equipped him to face the big, scary test of those hungry lions—both the peers who were attempting to destroy him as well as the big cats in the arena. Starting something small and then faithfully continuing it made his story so rich with meaning that it has been told for thousands of years now—and still counting.

1.5 AUTHOR AND FINISHER

How do you start something that will help you face the lions in your life? Or at least the occasional house cat? The best way to find a meaningful framework for your story is to pursue an eternal perspective. What story do you think God wants you to tell about your life? When you look into your future, where do you think God wants you to be? What does God want *you* to want? For now, don't worry about the distance between you and the end of your story; that could intimidate or even paralyze you. But you do need to think about where your future should be, so you can have some sense of what direction you need to start heading toward.

Chances are you can think of something right now that you know God would love to include in your story. Maybe you're strapped financially, but you know it would honor God for you to be able to tell the story of how you escaped from the bondage of debt to become a blessing to others. If Oseola McCarty's example inspired you, maybe you could change your story to something like this:

> Several years ago, I was drowning in debt. Then one day I decided to start a budget [or take a class or read a book or whatever is true to your story]. It wasn't easy, but I paid off first one credit card, then another. Before long, I paid off my car, then my student loans. Today I'm debt free except for the house, and I'm on track to have that paid off in less than four years. I don't just tithe anymore; my new financial freedom allows me to give generous offerings whenever I feel God's Spirit prompting me to.

Or maybe your story could involve changing your priorities. You know whether the story you're telling now is off track or headed in the wrong direction. But if you let God begin to author your story, it might one day go something like this:

Years ago I was so into my career that I was missing out on what was most important in life. I thought I was providing a better life for my family, but in reality I was pursuing selfish dreams and neglecting those I loved the most. That's when I decided to get home every evening by six o'clock [or stop taking work home or change careers or whatever is true to your story]. Now my marriage is better than it has ever been. I haven't missed one of my children's dance recitals or tee-ball games in over two years. This is the way life was supposed to be. Now I work to live, not the other way around.

It could be that you know you aren't properly caring for your body, the temple of the Spirit of God. You don't eat right. You rarely exercise. You are often stressed. You know God wants something different for you, so you decide to change your story. One day your story could be something like this:

When I realized I wasn't honoring God with my body, I decided to start working out daily [or hire a trainer or start a diet or begin walking or whatever is true to your story]. I know it's hard to believe, but I used to weigh about thirty pounds more than I do today. I feel better now than I ever have before.

Perhaps your family is a Christian family, but you aren't really growing in your faith or making a difference in this world. You know God wants more of your heart. Your story might go something like this:

Several years ago, we believed in God, but we didn't know him intimately, and we didn't serve him passionately. One day we decided to make God the top priority for our family. We committed to attend church [or join a small group or read the Bible together or get involved in a ministry or whatever is true to your story]. Now our whole family is centered on glorifying Christ in all we do. Our kids are bold in their faith. We're very involved in our church. And we can tell that we're making a difference serving every week in local ministry outreach. Now we don't just believe in God, but our lives revolve around serving him.

A small decision today could even impact your near future. It doesn't always take a long time to see big differences in your life. What story do you believe God wants you to tell five or ten years from now? What does God want you to want? Take a minute and jot down your thoughts. It doesn't have to be perfect. You don't have to commit to what you write just yet. Just capture on paper the first thoughts that come to mind.

1.6 JUST ONE THING

Now let's start connecting dots. This is where those daily small steps change your destination. And it's really pretty simple. Based on what you believe God wants you to want, what do you need to start? What discipline do you need to start doing to head toward where God wants you to get?

Notice that I asked not what disciplines (plural) but what discipline (singular). Choose only one thing. You'll be tempted to pick three, four, or even ten, but don't. Whatever you do, pick just one thing. Why are you limiting yourself to just one thing? Because if you pick more than one, you likely won't achieve any of them. But if you select just one God-directed discipline to start, you can begin writing the story God wants you to write.

For most of my adult life, I've started one new discipline each year. (You can start your one thing this year and then add another one thing next year.) While this may not seem like much change, over five years, I've added five new disciplines to my life. Over a decade, I've added ten. And each one is solidly locked in. While I'm still far from perfect, my life is richer and more enjoyable, and my story is closer to where God wants than it would be if I hadn't added these one things. Just imagine how different your story will be if over the next ten years you add ten God-centered disciplines to your life.

Let me share a few of the disciplines I started over the years and how they have changed my story. I grew up in a lower-middle-class home. We never went without the basics, but we never had a lot left over to help others. I decided that I wanted to have financial flexibility so our family could be generous to others. So in my early twenties, I set aside the first 10 percent of my income to give to God and the next 10 percent to invest.

Month after month, I put God first and invested in my future second. Many months this discipline was very difficult, but I never faltered. Investing 10 percent doesn't sound like a lot, especially when your income isn't much, and mine wasn't. But consistency over time with compounding interest made a difference. My small monthly investments added up—way up. Now we're able to live on a fraction of our income, debt free, giving freely—all because I decided to set aside a percentage of income early in life. My story is different because of this one small discipline.

Early in ministry, I found the hours of church work grueling. No matter how much I was doing, I always thought I could call on more people, train more volunteers, or study more for a message. I was convinced that I was too busy to take care of myself, so exercising was out of the question. Then one day a trusted mentor told me I didn't have time *not* to exercise. "If you don't take care of yourself," my mentor explained compassionately, "you won't be much good to others." So I decided to start working out. I picked a friend to join me. Now twenty years later, I still work out with the same friend, and I'm in good physical shape.

Like many people I know, I've always battled with working more than I should. Even though this behavior may be applauded by others who work with you, it is frowned on at home. Years ago I told my daughter I'd be home later to kiss her good night. She looked at me innocently and said, "Daddy, this isn't your home. You live at the office." That's when I decided to go to counseling for my workaholic tendencies. With the help of a good counselor, I've changed. One day when my children tell their story, I'll be a part of it because I've chosen to limit how much I work to focus on what matters most. This is a part of my story that I'll never regret.

Just two years after I became a Christian, I entered full-time ministry in the church. Consequently, I didn't know the Bible well at all. I was very insecure, constantly worried that how little I knew might be keeping me from helping people the way I should, and possibly even dishonoring God. I decid-ed to start reading through the Bible once each year. I can't remember how many years ago I started doing this. Now, I'm certainly no Bible scholar, but I do know the Bible a hundred times better today than if I had never started this discipline.

Thankfully, I was blessed with a good marriage right from the start. All of my friends know I married up—*way* up. And even though we've always been close, one day Amy told me that she desired more spiritual intimacy. Thanks to her encouragement, I decided we should start consistently praying together as a couple. (Believe it or not, this wasn't easy for me—and I'm a pastor!) But that one discipline made our good marriage even better. You'd be amazed how much God can change your marriage for the better when you seek him together daily.

I'd like to tell you about just one more "one thing." Several years ago, I noticed that ministry had become more of a strain on me than a joy. I felt like I was doing the work in my own strength, not depending on God, as I should. So I decided to devote the first twenty-one days of each new year to him, denying myself my normal food, fasting and seeking God. This wasn't just extremely difficult—at first, it was a great burden. But I cannot put into words how real the presence of God became to me through this process. For the last several years, our entire church staff has now joined me, along with many people who attend our church, in seeking God with a fast every January. More than just my story, the story of our entire church is now different because we decided to fast together.

Ever since I started seeking God through fasting, I can absolutely sense his voice more clearly. His Word is more alive to me than ever before. It even reveals to me things in my life that need to be cleansed.

Sometimes it's hard for me to keep track all of my feelings, everything I learn each day, and all of the questions I think of that I'd like to take to God. So this year, I decided I'd start journaling. I know a lot of people who have tried to journal, only to eventually give up. That won't happen to me. How do I know? Because I'm keeping it simple. I've committed to write at least one sentence a day. That's it. Just one sentence. So far, what I've found is that just one sentence can quickly lead to two, which then often flows into several paragraphs. But that's not the goal I set. By aiming for something achievable, I'm in the process of building yet another discipline that is helping shape the story that my life is telling today.

All of those one things become parts of my story. Don't let the thought of them overwhelm you. Big changes are possible; they just may not happen overnight. Remember, it's just a decision to start one thing each year. You can do that. With God's help, you know you can.

As I was writing this, I couldn't help reflecting on my choices. How much different would my life be if I had never decided to start those disciplines? What if I hadn't invested? I might be living paycheck to paycheck. What if I hadn't made exercise a priority? I might be overweight, out of shape, or worse. What if I hadn't got counseling for my problem of overworking? Would my family be in shambles today? What if Amy and I hadn't prayed together? Would we have drifted apart? Or worse? What if I hadn't made reading God's Word a daily priority? Who knows what I might have done to destroy my life? What if I hadn't fasted? Would I still be doing ministry in my own strength? Limiting what God wanted to do in me and through me?

1.7 READY, SET, START

There's an interesting story in the Old Testament about one of the leaders of Israel, King Ahab. A prophet explained that God would change the story of Israel by giving the enemy army into the hands of the Israelites. Ahab just couldn't see it. He asked, "But who will do this?"

The prophet answered him, "This is what the Lord says: 'The young officers of the provincial commanders will do it.'"

"And who will start the battle?" Ahab asked.

The prophet answered, "*You* will" (1 Kings 20:13–14, emphasis mine).

Think about the king's second question to the prophet: "Who will start the battle?" The prophet boldly replied, "You will!" If we want to see what God will accomplish, then we have to move toward him.

God will finish it, but you have to start it.

So what's your one thing? What one discipline do you need to start so that you can begin to write the story God wants you to write? You don't have to be stuck with the same story; you just have to do something different.

You might be dealing with a nagging insecurity, an addiction, or a fear. Maybe you need to start going to counseling or start memorizing Scripture or start making yourself accountable to a group.

Maybe you know you need to grow spiritually. Don't just think about it and feel bad about it. Do something about it. Start the ball moving. Perhaps you will commit to worship at church every week. Or maybe you'll decide to read through the Bible every year. Or you might join a small group or start serving in your church or start volunteering with a local missions group.

Do you need to grow as a leader? Improve as a mom? Grow as a husband? Maybe you should start learning from a mentor or start reading an article a week about the thing you want to get better at or begin praying daily about your need.

It might be that you need to get your finances under control. You're sick of swimming in debt, tired of worrying about money. Maybe it's time you start going to a Dave Ramsey class or get help creating a budget or start giving so you can break your grip on getting.

If your marriage isn't what it should be, what do you need to start so you can change the story of your marriage? Maybe it's time you start praying together daily or reading the Bible together or simply committing to going out alone once a week with no kids.

What one thing do you need to start?

If you know what it is, write it down now. Don't overthink this. Get it down on paper. Just write it down in a sentence or two.

If you have a lot of ideas and you're not sure where to start, I'm going to help you decide. Look at your phone or a clock and check the time. Did you do it? Good. Now, you have twenty-four hours to decide on one thing.

Think about it.

Pray about it.

Talk about it.

Sleep on it.

Briefly think some more tomorrow and then commit. You don't need weeks to come up with your one thing. By this time tomorrow, you will decide. And just like Daniel's decision to pray impacted the future story he'd tell, you'll begin writing the story that God wants you to tell.

Don't just think, "That's a great idea, Craig. It sounds really nice. I'll try that sometime," and then put it off.

There is no better time to start writing your future story than right now. The famous and very prolific Walt Disney said, "The way to get started is to quit talking and start doing." Today is a better day to start than tomorrow. If you don't start now, a year from now you'll wish you had.

Who's going to start it?

You will.

Start a discipline today that will change your story forever.

Just start where you are.

Just choose to take that first step.

Just one step.

#Struggles DVD Study

Following Jesus in a Selfie-Centered World

Craig Groeschel

We all love the benefits of technology and social media, but even with the incredible upsides, many of us suspect there are unintended negative consequences beyond our control. The more we compare ourselves with others, the less satisfied we are. The more we interact online, the more we crave face-to-face intimacy. The more filtered our lives become, the more challenging it is for us to be authentic. The more information we receive about the pain and crises in the world, the more difficult it is for us to care.

In this timely five-session video-based study (study guide sold separately or with the kit), *New York Times* bestselling author Craig Groeschel taps in to some of the most up-to-date studies on social media to help us understand how it affects our emotions, our relationships, our attitudes, and our beliefs. He offers real-life examples to reveal the depths to which each of us battles with social media, how it masks our real struggles, and how we can reclaim a Christ-centered life. He encourages us to regain control over our lives by rediscovering the principles real life with Jesus brings: contentment, intimacy, authenticity, compassion, and rest.

#Struggles will show you the ways technology has enslaved you rather than served you and what changes your need to make in your life to restore balance. Above all, it will point you to Christ and help you understand the healing he wants to do in you. As you follow his leading and seek him first, you will find you are no longer defined by *who follows you* but by *the one you follow.*

From This Day Forward

Five Commitments to Fail-Proof Your Marriage

Craig Groeschel and Amy Groeschel

Five commitments to fail-proof your marriage
Everyone dreams of a fairy-tale marriage—the perfect spouse, the perfect home, the perfect family. But reality tells us that these expectations don't hold up very long.

Many studies indicate that close to fifty percent of marriages don't make it. With those odds, is it even possible to have a good marriage—let alone a great one? *New York Times* bestselling author and pastor Craig Groeschel insists you can ... but not if you approach it like everyone else does.

Craig and his wife, Amy, show single adults and married couples how to conquer the odds and find the joy, passion, and strength of a marriage built by God.

Craig and Amy open their hearts, share personal experiences, and walk you through five powerful commitments you can make to fail-proof your marriage:

1. Seek God.
2. Fight fair.
3. Have fun.
4. Stay pure.
5. Never give up.

If you earnestly choose to do all five of these things, you will discover a richer, deeper, more authentic marriage.

Starting right now—from this day forward.

Fight
Winning the Battles That Matter Most

Craig Groeschel

Some Battles Are Worth Fighting For

Author and pastor Craig Groeschel helps you uncover who you really are—a powerful man with the heart of a warrior. With God's help, you'll find strength to fight the battles you know you must win: the ones that determine the state of your heart, the quality of your marriage, and the spiritual health of those you love most.

Craig examines the life of Samson—a strong man with glaring weaknesses. Like many men, Samson taunted his enemy and rationalized his sins. The good news is God's grace is greater than your worst sin. By looking at Samson's life, you'll learn to defeat the demons that make strong men weak. You'll tap into a strength you never knew was possible. You'll become who God made you to be—a man who knows how to fight for what's right.

Don't just fight like a man. Fight like a man of God.
For God's Sake ... FIGHT

Hardcover, Printed Caseside: 978-0-310-33374-6

Soul Detox

Clean Living in a Contaminated World

Craig Groeschel

   As standards of conduct continue to erode in our shock-proof world, we must fight the soul pollution threatening our health, our faith, and our witness to others. Without even knowing it, people willingly inhale secondhand toxins, poisoning their relationship with God and stunting their spiritual growth.

   Soul Detox examines the toxins that assault us daily, including toxic influences, toxic emotions, and toxic behaviors.

   By examining the toxins that assault us daily, this book offers the ultimate spiritual intervention with ways to remain clean, pure, and focused on the standard of God's holiness.

   Hardcover, Jacketed: 978-0-310-33368-5
   Small Group Curriculum Also Available:
   5-Session DVD—9780310894919
   Study Guide—9780310687528
   Study Guide with DVD—9780310685760

WEIRD
Because Normal Isn't Working

Craig Groeschel, author of
The Christian Atheist

Normal people are stressed, overwhelmed, and exhausted. Many of their relationships are, at best, strained and, in most cases, just surviving. Even though we live in one of the most prosperous places on earth, normal is still living paycheck to paycheck and never getting ahead. In our oversexed world, lust, premarital sex, guilt, and shame are far more common than purity, virginity, and a healthy married sex life. And when it comes to God, the majority believe in him, but the teachings of Scripture rarely make it into their everyday lives.

Simply put, normal isn't working.

Groeschel's *Weird* views will help you break free from the norm to lead a radically abnormal (and endlessly more fulfilling) life.

Small Group Curriculum Also Available:
6-Session DVD—9780310894971
Study Guide—9780310894986
Study Guide with DVD—9780310684305
Hardcover, Jacketed: 978-0-310-32790-5

The Christian Atheist

Believing in God but Living as if He Doesn't Exist

Craig Groeschel

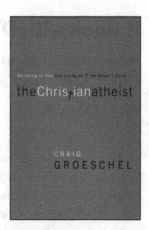

> "The more I looked, the more I found Christian Atheists everywhere."

Former Christian Atheist Craig Groeschel knows his subject all too well. After more than a decade of successful ministry, he had to make a painful self-admission: although he believed in God, he was leading his church as if God didn't exist.

To Christians and non-Christians alike, to the churched and the unchurched, the journey leading up to Groeschel's admission and the journey that follows—from his family and his upbringing to the lackluster and even diametrically opposed expressions of faith he encountered—will look and sound like the story of their own lives.

Groeschel's personal journey toward a more authentic God-honoring life is more relevant than ever.

Christians and Christian Atheists everywhere will be nodding their heads as they are challenged to ask, Am I putting my whole faith in God but still living as if everything were up to me?

Hardcover, Jacketed: 978-0-310-32789-9
Small Group Curriculum Also Available:
6-Session DVD—9780310329794
Study Guide—9780310329756
Study Guide with DVD—9780310494300

Available in stores and online!

It Book with DVD

How Churches and Leaders Can Get It and Keep It

Craig Groeschel

Pack containing one book and one DVD. When Craig Groeschel founded LifeChurch.tv, the congregation met in a borrowed two-car garage, with ratty furnishings and faulty audiovisual equipment. But people were drawn there, sensing a powerful, life-changing force Groeschel calls "It." What is It, and how can you and your ministry get—and keep—It? Combining in-your-face honesty with off-the-wall humor, this book tells how any believer can obtain It, get It back, and guard It. One of today's most innovative church leaders, Groeschel provides profile interviews with Mark Driscoll, Perry Noble, Tim Stevens, Mark Batterson, Jud Wilhite, and Dino Rizzo. This lively book and DVD will challenge churches and their leaders to maintain the spiritual balance that results in experiencing It in their lives.

Mixed Media Set: 978-0-310-49318-1

Available in stores and online!